Dharma's Daughters

Dharma's Daughters

Contemporary Indian Women and Hindu Culture

◆ ◆ ◆

SARA S. MITTER

RUTGERS UNIVERSITY PRESS

New Brunswick, New Jersey

The lines from the poem "Stings" by Sylvia Plath, quoted as the epigraph to chapter 6, are from her collection *Ariel*, copyright © 1963 by Ted Hughes, reprinted by permission of Harper & Row Publishers, Inc. Acknowledgment is made to Sidgwick & Jackson, Publishers, for permission to quote from A. L. Basham's translations of the *Rig-Veda, Mahabharata, Laws of Manu,* and *Lay of the Anklet* in *The Wonder That Was India* (1959).

Library of Congress Cataloging-in-Publication Data

Mitter, Sara S., 1938–
Dharma's daughters : contemporary Indian women and Hindu culture / Sara S. Mitter.
p. cm.
Includes bibliographical references and index.
ISBN 0-8135-1677-3
1. Women—Indian—Bombay—Social conditions. 2. Women, Hindu—India—Bombay. 3. Feminism—India—Bombay. 4. Bombay (India)—Social conditions. I. Title.
HQ1745.B65M58 1991
305.42'0954'7923—dc20 90-19387
CIP

British Cataloging-in-Publication information available

Manufactured in the United States of America

In memory of my mother,
to my two belles-mères,
and for my father

Contents

PART THREE

Preface

Indian women have intrigued me for twenty years. Several are relatives: I am the American daughter-in-law of a Bengali family. I am always welcomed home in India with openness and affection. Yet, for a long time, little about that country, that world, made sense to me.

I had no India mystique as a buffer: quite the contrary. India began for me in January 1975, on the dreadful night ride from Dum Dum airport into Calcutta, when I first brought my son and baby daughter home to their grandmother. The auspicious arrival of the daughter-in-law was hailed by servants standing in the driveway sounding conch shells in the sulphurous Calcutta night.

From that first immersion I came out all exclamation points. My letters bristled; my notebooks bulged with grim stories clipped from newspapers. Nights I'd stay up writing everything down because during the day I had no one to talk to: only my kinfolk turning themselves inside out with hospitality and my small children, stuffed with milk sweets and too young to pose questions.

Subsequent visits modified my perceptions and broadened my outlook, but they did not ease my puzzlement. Short visits gave way to longer ones, and what first seemed exotic interludes became integral parts of my real life. In the fall of 1985, I arrived for a year's stay in Bombay with my husband and daughter. They both had programs set out for them: physics research for one, junior high school for the other. As a Bombay homemaker, I joined ranks with the women whom I had long watched covertly, sometimes admiring, sometimes appalled. Well-situated as an inside-outsider, I set out to learn more about urban Indian women's lives.

The timing was right. For some years, India had been looking less alien, less problematical to ordinary Western eyes. Magazine photos no longer featured gaunt faces and outstretched hands; they now showed thriving marketplaces and glamorous vacation spots. Publicity campaigns projected artistry and elegance, not the India of the cheap striped bedcover you once bought for your college dorm. Vast and various, a free country—the world's largest democracy, after all—a goods-hungry market was abuilding, and a talented, resourceful people was striding ahead into the twenty-first century.

And what about the women? Classically photogenic in either their opulence or their distress, Indian women have often been pictured, but rarely revealed. Our knowledge of the lives they lead is largely anecdotal; it comes from stereotyped images, some exotic notions, a few grim facts. How are Indian women experiencing the accelerated momentum of the march toward modernity? How do the classic images of Indian womanhood fit with the changing orientations of the "new" India? How is Indian society responding to the new demands and widening horizons of women?

Western travelers are always in search of a personal India. They trek the highlands, ride the railways, paddle down sacred and profaned rivers, abide in the holy places. For me, the significant landscape was the Third World metropolis, with its masses of female figures. My observation post was greater Bombay, India's fastest-paced city, where many ethnicities, languages, and religions coexist. Immense in its size, its problems, and its ambitions, Bombay is quintessentially Indian, but no more a "typical" Indian city—there is no such thing—than New York is typical of the United States.

A word about my vantage point. The predominantly Hindu women in these pages are seen from different distances. Those with whom I had no common language are simply observed, others are encountered, and still others are evidently peers, colleagues, friends. This limitation also confers an advantage. By bringing literate Hindu women into close-up, I hope to kindle in the reader a recognition of affinities and to encourage a sense of rapport that field study samples do not often provide.

A number of people helped make this project possible. I am grateful to the Kentucky Foundation for Women for a grant for a month's follow-up travel and research. Everyone I interviewed in India gave generously of her time and interest. My thanks to Indu Balagopal, M.D., of Mobile Creches, Niloufer Bhagwat, attorney-at-law, Kiran Bhatia of Sanjivini, Subhadra Butalia of Karmika, Neera Desai and Vibhuti Patel of Shrimati Nathibai Damodar Thackersey (SNDT) University, Madhu Kishwar, Prema Purao of Annapurna Mahila Mandal, Kalpana Sharma, the staff of the Institute of Social Studies Trust, Saheli Women's Resource Center, and staff members of the Self Employed Women's Association.

I am particularly indebted to the gracious friends and neighbors whom I have drawn upon for the composite portraits in chapters 1, 2, 4, 6, and 15. All names are fictitious.

To the friends who variously provided hospitality, invaluable criticism, research help, or quiet work space at crucial moments, I am most grateful. They include Aditya and Lolita Nehru, T. R. and Jayashree Ramadas, Laura Maslow-Armand, Marie-France Hanseler, and Françoise Leenhardt.

Warm thanks to my supportive family: Anjali, who made the best of being hauled off to Bombay without being asked, Siddhartha, for his affection and encouragement, and Pronob, who is at the root of it.

Paris, October 1990

Note: Rupee amounts cited in the text are based on the exchange rate at the time of writing: Rs 17 = $1 US. The rate in early 1991 was Rs 19= $1 US.

Dharma's Daughters

Introduction

THIS BOOK is an inquiry into the lives of contemporary urban Indian women. The approach, for so multifarious a subject, is akin to that of a documentary film: live reportage, background research, and interpretation, with the aim of projecting images of individuals and groups that fairly suggest the larger picture.

The book is divided into three sections. Part One presents some women who live and work in the city of Bombay. They include manual laborers, illiterate domestic workers, home-based producers living in shanties and tenements, and educated middle-class women of two generations—one born around the time of Independence (1947), and one coming of age today. My intention in grouping these six chapters is twofold: to convey something of the texture of life in one major city of the developing world, and to consider some implications for women as mothers and homemakers, as wage earners, as private individuals, as prospective wives.

Part Two introduces the elements of Hindu myth and tradition that help foster the conditions to which most women's lives are subject. Although India is secular and pluralistic, Hindu cultural patterns going back four thousand years deeply affect all the minority groups—Muslim, Christian, Parsi—perhaps nowhere more conspicuously than in matters relating to the position of women. I discuss the pertinence of Hindu lore to daily living and the often abusive interpretations of tradition with regard to women.

Part Three tells of resistance, the rising defiance and mobilization of Indian women since the 1970s. I present a brief history of the women's movement and examples of working women's cooperatives, self-help associations, and resource centers. In the context of India's current state of social evolution, I look at some pressures that today are propelling women in the directions of either accommodation or resistance.

These pressures are not felt by women alone, of course, but by the whole society. At their source, two factors predominate. One, the most ancient and potent, is Hinduism—a faith, a mentality, and a social institution all in one. The other is modernization, the accelerating agricultural and industrial growth and urbanization of the country. While producing vast improvements, modernization places unprecedented strains on the traditional social fabric, as greater numbers of men and women find themselves in situations not covered by the old understandings.

Any comprehension of things Indian, from the most sublime bronze statues to the spittle-wads on the pavement, requires some acquaintance with the Hindu worldview. This basis, the invisible primer coat, imbues the whole canvas. Here one does not so much mean the abstractions of Hindu philosophy, but rather the popular interpretations and norms of conduct. Many of these have long been accepted or assimilated by the non-Hindu (largely Muslim) minority, and many practices that have been challenged by civil law owe their impunity to convergences in Hindu and Muslim attitudes and traditions.

The individual in Hindu society is from the womb secured in a pattern of relationships, social and spiritual obligations, and eventual rewards. These are inculcated by one's kinfolk, reinforced by clan and community, and perpetually represented in art, mythology, and popular culture. The Hindu deities, their avatars, and certain epic heroes and heroines incarnate the tradition and transmit the message. Unlike their cousins the progeny of Zeus, they are not merely historical. They are alive and well and living just about everywhere: in wondrously intricate carved temples, in street-corner tree hollows, on *paan* stalls (a popular chew made of betel leaf, lime, and aromatics) and photocopy booths, on taxi dashboards and truck tailgates. Their prodigious feats are the staple of mass-market movies and best-selling comic books. Even in Christian homes, Hindu culture is often present: the framed lithograph of pale Jesus in his blue robes is likely to be flanked by the rotund elephant-headed Ganesh, remover of obstacles and bringer of wealth and good fortune.

An eminent virtue of Hinduism over its four-thousand-year history has been its capacity to integrate heterodox elements, rather than proscribe or launch holy wars against them. Seemingly aberrant ideas are tolerated as being possibly valid alternative paths to the same end, enlightenment: liberation from the illusory grip of the everyday. Thus, over the centuries, many apparent anomalies have been absorbed into the living tradition of Hinduism. One such is the equivocal image of the woman. Another is Hinduism's broad tolerance of, verging on indifference to, the Other—persons outside one's own clan or caste-determined community. Accepting or respecting another's chosen way of life may mean offering bed and board to a derelict ascetic. It may also help assure the invisibility of the sidewalk beggar, not holy, just starving. He is as entitled to squat and grovel outside the overpriced, over–air-conditioned restaurant as we are to step over him on our way to overeat inside.

Western minds, used to thinking in terms of this *or* that, but not this *as well as* that, may find in the wide latitude and moral relativism of Hinduism a deviousness or downright lack of principle; and they may see a logical outgrowth of this in the cheating and corruption that touch all levels of political and economic life. Yet one great merit of the Hindu way is its freedom from dogmatism and pretensions to an exclusive "revealed" Truth. Historically, Hinduism has been capable of generating new interpretations in the interest of social reform.

The image-worshiping rites and sometimes lurid ceremonies of popular cults can contribute to sensory onslaught and general bewilderment. Yet Hindu philosophy is sober and profound, unflinchingly contemplating the immensities of time and space and yet minutely cataloguing the goals of human life—how they are to be attained and what must be avoided along the way. *Dharma*, the Eternal Way, the totality of social, ethical, and spiritual harmony, orchestrates the whole. Dharma is at the same time the eternal law of the universe and the virtuous path of each individual.

What keeps these two aspects—eternal law and personal

accountability—aligned and even convergent are two bedrock assumptions. First, through the strict, detailed, *hierarchic* ordering of all human endeavor each individual, type of work, and range of conduct have places and values in a vast world order, extending through countless reincarnations. And second, the *patriarchal* principle governs the functioning of home, workplace, and community. Together these tenets legitimize caste divisions, reinforce social inequalities, and necessarily assign inferior status to the female.

The condition of women was at a low ebb in the 1700s, when India began to pass from Moghul domination to British control. Politically fragmented and economically weak, India had been mired in its sluggish rural economy and archaic traditions. Ideas, institutions, and social relations were as slow to evolve as were the means of production. Indian and British reformers led vigorous crusades against child marriage, widow immolation, and other medieval practices. But even in the late 1800s, girls had little formal schooling (upper-class young ladies might be tutored at home), were likely to be married off at or before puberty, and became nonpersons if widowed, whatever their age.

With the increased industrialization and rising demand for self-rule that marked the early twentieth century, the better educated, more affluent and mobile sectors began to experience a "wrong fit" between traditional assumptions and modern conditions. Thousands of upper-caste women identified with and were galvanized by Gandhi's campaign for home rule. Well before independence was in the air, Gandhi made certain that political equality for women be written into the Congress party program.

In 1949, the constitution that established India as a democratic, secular nation outlawed all forms of discrimination against previously second-class citizens—that is, former untouchables, religious minorities, and women. The principle of universal equality before the law ran counter to some deeply held beliefs. But specific acts of legislation gave women equal or near-equal inheritance rights and amended the marriage and divorce laws to allow women to initiate divorce and demand child custody. Legal abortion followed, for reasons of population control, not in the context of women's rights.

Thus, on paper, female citizens were subject to the law of the land, as interpreted by the courts, not by religious conclaves or patriarchal councils. In practice, of course, many old inequities persist quite undisturbed.

Today in India there is much talk about imminent modernity. Visions of the early twenty-first century—when the population will exceed one billion—foresee conquest of poverty, annihilation of illiteracy, last-ditch conservation of ravaged natural resources, effective family planning, uplift of backward tribes. These miracles are to be achieved by the existing political parties and their perennial chieftains, most of whom are invested in preserving the status quo and the stereotype of the selfless Indian wife and mother, goddess of the home. No established political leader or mass-based party has seriously questioned whether the patriarchal and hierarchic structures are adapted to attaining these grand, quasi-immediate goals.

Perhaps available evidence has not yet been striking enough to raise such unsettling questions. In recent years, the state-regulated but essentially free-enterprise economy has been lurching ahead satisfactorily. Capitalist expansion proceeds hand in hand with existing feudal values. The highly elaborated organization of Hinduism provides an effective brake. Patriarchy holds back labor movements; hierarchy and casteism support a system of differential advantages. Both encourage class exploitation, inhibit protest, and reinforce the traditional roles of daughters and wives.

Yet the situation grows more precarious in direct proportion to its success. An overloaded truck with bald tires and worn brake linings—an everyday sight by way of analogy—may be a viable carrier on known routes at modest speeds, but not when driven like a juggernaut. Each day in India, the number and variety of outrages and catastrophes reported in the press boggle the imagination. But the drivers, the professional politicians and the moneyed elite, are clinging to the steering wheel for dear life.

Yes, but . . . everyone knows that India looks like that, chaos abounding. The definitive calamity never happens. Technological innovation grafted onto backwardness only makes for more colorful juxtapositions. One newspaper column reveals official hush-ups of leaks in a deuterium plant. The adjacent column carries an item about how seven women drowned when the bullock cart in which they were traveling tried to overtake another bullock cart and fell into an irrigation ditch. Curiously such contrasts seem an integral element in the stability. They illustrate how unevenly distributed are the benefits of development. A trickling-down effect is discernible further and further down the scale, but the disparities between have and have-not groups, castes, and regions persist or amplify. And whatever the level of deprivation or oppression of a family or community, the women's lot is systematically grimmer than the men's. This is widely regarded as normal—that is, eternally and immutably the case.

Yet the routine devaluation of women in a society that is either unable to recognize it or able, at best, to offer fatalistic justifications has become a flaming issue. Since the early 1970s, women from all walks of life have been taking up arms: indigenous, ingenious instruments for change. Their legendary patience seems to have a limit after all.

In these same years, social scientists in India and in the West have been looking more closely at the socialization of females in India and at the prevailing images and self-images of women. This rich research is not readily available to nonspecialists. Nor does one find much echo of it in a press still avid for tales of a young widow ablaze on her husband's pyre or the colorful mass wedding of six- and eight-year-olds.

This book is offered as a cordial attempt to redress the balance.

Part One

◆ 1 ◆

THE DANCE OF MAYURI

Like the streets of New York, the streets of Bombay abound with women. They are dressed in sari or skirt and blouse, in *salwar kameez* (tunic and ankle-hugging trousers) or jeans. Some cover their hair; a few are veiled. They are out shopping or doing errands; they are pouring out of trains and buses and hurrying to work. Before dawn, the influx begins, with factory workers, then the fisherwomen and market women. Later come the civil servants, the secretaries and bank clerks, teachers and salespeople. And there are throngs of students, Hindu, Parsi, Christian, Muslim: Miss Kelkar, Miss Batliwalla, Miss D'Mello, Miss Hussain.

There are others, of course, many others. Walking in the city streets, you will step around a woman cooking supper on the pavement while her tiny children play with a tin cup and chips of broken paving stone. Waiting for the bus, you will be able to study women scavengers hulking full gunny sacks along the gutter. At an outdoor market, you can observe a woman bargaining for a little bunch of grapes with two rupees she has managed to economize from her week's shopping allowance. In the lending library, you may overhear two women selecting four-rupee magazines they can afford to borrow for a few *paise,* but not to buy. (There are one hundred paise in a rupee, whose 1990 value is about six cents.)

In the smart boutique, at the taxi stand, in the pastry shoppe of the five-star hotel, you will see pale, padded women, and hear their particular tone of voice, querulous and imperious. Standing in a packed bus, conversing in the post office queue, visiting their offices or their living rooms, you can gather impressions of the lives of women over a spectrum that, in Bombay, is about as wide as it can get.

◆ ◆ ◆

A day or two after I'd begun to get settled, Gita invited me to come view *Mayuri*, a mass-market Indian movie with a topical twist. The videotape was hers for a day, on loan from the star, who was in Bombay on a promotion tour. Gita is a freelance magazine and newspaper writer. She did not own a VCR, but had no problem finding a neighbor willing to project the film on hers.

When I arrived at five o'clock at the twelfth-floor apartment, a dozen women were already seated decorously in a semicircle of straight-backed chairs. A servant girl drew the heavy curtains against the glaring October sunlight, and the film began. The dialogue was in Tamil, the mother tongue of most of the women present. Two lines of subtitles, Hindi and English, flickered brokenly on the screen.

The plot was based on a remarkable true story. Mayuri, a beautiful, talented college girl, sets her heart on becoming a classical dancer. Many odds must be overcome before she triumphs in her first solo recital. Then comes disaster: an automobile accident that results in the amputation of her lower leg. Though chastened, she cannot give up her passion for the dance. Eventually she comes to learn of the "Jaipur foot," a flexible prosthesis developed by an Indian doctor. Through willpower, grueling effort, and faith in the lord Shiva, she manages not only to walk but also to dance again. In the film, Mayuri plays herself. If there is any doubt about the footwork, it is dispelled when she pulls her sari up above the knee and unstraps the painted leg and decorated rubber foot.

To extend the film's appeal, the facts are heavily dosed with *masala*—spiced up. The car accident is the fault of a callow, self-indulgent boyfriend in whom the pure-hearted Mayuri had naively placed her trust. There is a henpecked father, a mean stepmother, a providential granny, a vulgar "other woman," and the repentant—but ultimately despicable—boyfriend. Prayers are answered by the timely appearance of a deus ex machina. And, as in all commercial Indian films, the plot frequently halts for song and dance numbers, glittering and glamorous.

But there is a message. Mayuri triumphs as both a dancer

and a free woman. The final shots show her performing for herself in her own spacious apartment. She sways from window to window, slamming the shutters one by one on the pleading face of her rekindled lover. Singing her liberty, she shuts him out.

The film ran on for nearly three hours. During this time, the sun blazed orange, deepened to blood red, and sank into the calm Arabian Sea. At some point the servant girl pulled back the drapes and opened the windows onto the glimmering, deepening sky. The room grew dark.

Attentive and reserved, the women sat with never a fidget nor a comment. From time to time, Sonali V., our hostess, went either to the kitchen where the whoosh of a pressure cooker could be heard or to the bedroom to admonish some children. The room where we sat contained a leatherette sofa and assorted chairs, a formica dining table, the refrigerator, and three mounted shelves displaying whatnots and souvenirs. There were no pictures, no bookcases, no plants, no decor. The room had a single axis. In the alcove stood the television set on its pedestal, mounted by the VCR. Diagonally opposite, on a low table just behind us, was a glass-encased two-foot-high bronze statue of the four-armed dancing god, Shiva Nataraj. Around the base lay fresh garlands of jasmine and marigold.

Halfway through the screening, Mr. V. came home. He passed through the darkened room without a word. A few minutes later, he reappeared in casual shirt and trousers. His wife gave him her chair. She sat for a few moments on the floor, then went to the kitchen. In the dim room, the husband half turned in the chair, moving his head, seeking her. When she came back, he shifted his weight, making a slight movement of his neck and shoulders. She brought a cushion and placed it for his back.

Now Mayuri's drama was nearing its peak. In a saffron sari framed by wooden crutches, she is visiting a playground with her friend, a happily married housewife, and the friend's small child. Watching all the capering tots becomes too much for Mayuri, and she falters in her stoic submission to her fate. She leans against a tree to weep. "Pray. Turn to your god," the friend counsels.

The hobbling dancer delivers up her prayer with such fervid devotion that she nearly faints. Psychedelic images whirl on the screen. Gently, the friend takes her hand. They watch a little boy challenge his father to follow him up the rungs of the jungle gym. The father takes such disproportionate pride in doing so that the two young women can't help but make an amused comment. "You think I am foolish," says the gentleman. "But no! I am not whole-bodied like you." And he rolls his trouser up to display the miracle prosthesis.

Shiva Nataraj! At that moment, Mr. V. half rose and turned in his chair. His wife stood forward from her leaning position against the wall, and they exchanged a long, intimate, affirmative look.

Freshly arrived as I was on the scene, I retained many images from that afternoon. The strongest were not of the film but of the room, high above a shanty colony at the eastern edge of the Arabian Sea: the worthy women, each with a long plait of black hair, or a sensible bun; the grace of the young servant girl with her dancer's top-knot and flounced, ankle-length skirt, rising on tiptoe to arrange the curtains, her silhouette eloquent against the pale sky; the presence of deity and ceremony in the household.

Behind the reserved manner and obliging smiles of the women, I sensed mysteries. The sensuousness and glamour of the sari, with its tight molding bodice and long silky drape, contrasted with the Sunday-go-to-meeting demeanor of the sari-wearers. I felt shy with these women, as though I'd crashed a gathering of alumnae of an old-fashioned girls' academy. Except for Gita, I did not know anyone personally. I knew that they were all housewives and mothers, born around the time of the birth of independent India. They had grown up in conservative middle-class Hindu families in provincial cities like Tanjore and Madras. Most of them were married young, in the customary manner, by arrangement between families of the same caste-community. Soon after marriage, the husband's career brought them to Bombay, where Marathi is the official tongue and a kind of Hindi cockney is spoken.

In many respects, these women's life experiences differed significantly from those of their mothers. And their short-haired, blue-jeaned daughters seemed to be accomplishing a further transition. Yet Sonali and her neighbors were assiduous performers of wifely and domestic duties that they perceived not very differently from the way their mothers had. Prudent and resourceful homemakers, they were not given to splurges, flights of fancy, or stirrings of revolt. Was there something in Mayuri's struggle and achievement that spoke to them? Or had they just come for a movie, curious, and glad of a break in an unvarying routine?

Once again I confronted the question that plagued me each time I was in India. The way that women lived their lives in Hindu society was enigmatic: so conventional in the external aspects, and internally so complex. Previous visits in Calcutta and Bombay had given me a notion of the constraints imposed on women by the physical surroundings, economic realities, and social imperatives. But my curiosity tugged at the edges of a greater mystery. The Woman Question is a persistent ambiguity, the status of women a paradox at the very heart of Hindu culture. It is manifest in over twenty centuries of ritual art, where lavish sculpted bodies in explicit erotic play are intended to lift the viewer toward increased spirituality and liberation from desire. The mystery abides in the religion: an austere godhead and patriarchal host are sidelined by an array of female deities who are ardently feared and adored. The question underlies the structure of daily life. Woman, worshiped as goddess and exalted as mother, is, in most practical aspects of life, overworked and undervalued, systematically subordinated. Not only among the pious or in the backward sectors of society does this duality operate, but its manifestations also occur all the way up to the top. Women themselves tend the flame of patriarchal traditions, taking care that inequality be maintained. Yet Indian history is marked by the emergence of powerful, self-directed,and charismatic women.

In sum, the cultural construct of woman, and the life of every woman starting before her birth, seem riven with contradictions more blatant *and* more subtle than those affecting women of North America and Western Europe. Such contradictions are sometimes viewed as pertaining to the conflict between tradition and modernity. For a tradition-oriented, family-subsumed woman like Sonali, husband, home, and heritage are the prime sources of identity and emotional fulfillment. For Gita, and for the personage of Mayuri, a transition is in process from ritual patterns of acquiescence to a new affirmation of self.

It is probably more accurate to suggest that in many women, both orientations are at work or at war. This is not just a middle-class predicament because the behavior of this sector is widely emulated and determines the patterns to which lower social groups aspire. It is also not a new conflict. A few generations back, only a small privileged minority felt concerned, but their experience was already significant enough to be studied in depth. [1] Today, the existence of competing norms and models, each valid in its own terms, is recognized as just another fact of life—one more thing that one must deal with, making decisions as the need arises, with greater or lesser consistency. Indian women are well practiced in this: they have too little time in the day and too much to do to shilly-shally. Most wives and homemakers, whether home is a hovel or a tidy apartment, expect a great deal from themselves—and not much help from the menfolk, the environment, or the powers that be.

Two phrases occurred repeatedly in my conversations with women at disparate social and economic levels: "You get used to it." "Somehow, I managed." The assurance, satisfaction, and pride in their voices provide a gauge of their strength and their susceptibility.

◆ 2 ◆

THE WOMEN'S COMPARTMENT

Girl should be pretty, well-educated, with modern outlook moderated with traditional values, and be able to adjust to a close-knit family.

—Matrimonial advertisement in The Times of India

The first time I boarded a Western Railway local at Churchgate Station, I had no idea how many stops there would be before we reached the suburb of Santa Cruz. From where I sat, squeezed among eight other women on a wooden bench meant for six, I could see nothing of the stations we passed. The small, barred windows were set just below eye level, seemingly intended for ventilation, not for looking out or being looked in upon. The car had two sets of open doorways, with no doors. In the brief stops, the two-way surge of bodies was such that I could neither make out what was on the platform nor catch sight of a readable station sign. At some stops, everyone piled out the right-hand exit; at others, the action happened on the left.

Later, I knew the stations by their look, by the density of the crowd, by the smell; but that first time, I began to feel nervous. I relinquished my seat and started to push toward the doorways. Looking for someone who was sure to speak English, I spotted a young woman dressed in a yellow- and plum-colored designer version of the traditional salwar-kameez, the type of outfit sold in the chic boutiques of Bandra. Her hair, not middle-parted and confined in a braid, was cut short and styled loosely around her face. Kamla saw me checking her out and answered my question almost before it was asked. She was also going to Santa Cruz, about a forty-five minute ride.

We stood clutching two of the wooden handles hanging from leather straps above our heads. Not everyone is tall enough to reach them or sufficiently unencumbered by bags or babies. Those who aren't just sway, or grab for the nearest arm or shoulder when the train veers. We were in one of the women's compartments. Women passengers are free to ride in any wagon, but two or three are reserved for us. The choice comes down to which gender you least mind being wedged against and stampeded by and in which company you feel you have a fighting chance of a little breathing space. Bombay commuter trains have virtually no off-peak hour. During main peak hours, each nine-car "rake," as they are called, carries 3,500 to 4,000 passengers, as against a "crush capacity"—projected maximum load—of 2,600. And this is despite the fact that, on the Western Railway out of Churchgate and the Central and Harbour lines out of Victoria Terminus, trains arrive and depart every three minutes.

While I exchanged small talk with Kamla, I became aware of another difference between this train and other metropolitan systems that I knew, like the Boston T or the Paris RER. It was the human noise level. High-pitched chatter was going on all around. Had they all boarded in companionable twos and threes? No. Simply, every rider was a ready participant in the small dramas of the journey: prompt to take sides if two women began to argue over a seat or a leaning place; commiserating with or pooh-poohing complainers; cajoling a sniveling child or a crying baby. Above this mild din of gynaeceum wafted the cries of female peddlers hawking cheap trinkets—stick-on beauty marks, plastic combs, barrettes, bangles, fresh jasmine garlands for the hair. These scruffy, weather-beaten girls of indeterminate age whined their way along the nonexistent aisles, not without heated exchanges with legitimate passengers and competing hawkers. Some were trailed by younger barefoot sisters and brothers, toting a box of hairpins; but basically they were just along for the ride, and there was no one to look after them at home, whatever home was.

The train began to traverse a fetid smell reminiscent of the New Jersey turnpike in its most odoriferous days, and I saw we were on a causeway crossing the scum-covered marshes and rubbish-strewn wastes of Mahim Creek. Somewhere off to the right lay Dharavi, said to be the biggest single slum in all Asia. Then we left the stink behind and pulled into Bandra. A number of light-complexioned, well-dressed women moved toward the doorway. The high school girls packed away their study guides and movie magazines, calling farewells to each other in fluted, cadenced English. Their parochial-school pinafores strained to censor their truly classic charms.

Until a year ago, Kamla had also been in snuff-colored jumper and school tie, but now she could dress as she pleased. She was nearly seventeen and in her first year of college, which, in the local education system, corresponds to our eleventh grade. Kamla had attended a girls' school run by a Catholic order. Now she was enrolled in a coed institution and circulated daily in Bombay, without having to account for her goings and comings. The youngest of four children, she was heir to the concessions that had been hard won by her elder siblings. Yet Kamla was what mothers call a nice, sensible girl, not a tester or questioner. We met several times that autumn, to exchange competencies. She coached me in simple Hindi conversation, and I tried to undo the damage done in her two years of ill-taught French. In the process, I learned something of her family history.

Kamla's mother had produced two daughters, Vimla and Tanya; then she miscarried and ceased to conceive. After two years, magic ritual in the form of offerings and self-purifications was summoned to the aid of medical science. A "very respected" astrologer was consulted. He predicted a male birth, but his ambiguous language raised fears that the precious son would be handicapped, a "special gift." Arjun was born a normal male baby. The gift followed: Kamla, conceived an indecently short time after the forty-day postpartum period, arrived in the same calendar year as her brother.

This was interpreted as part of a package deal of sorts, as if Kamla, the predestined third in the all-girl family, had briefly postponed her arrival to allow for the workings of grace. It seems likely that the mother, weary of delphic prophecies, chose then to have herself sterilized.

As a child, Kamla was like a mascot or lucky charm. She was spared the expectations that were placed upon, and perfectly fulfilled by, her eldest sister Vimla and then ringingly challenged by Tanya. Vimla was one of those docile, exquisite creatures who seem to exist to confirm myths about Indian women and to demonstrate why some European men seek brides through the Indian matrimonial columns. She had flawless skin, perfect teeth, and a modest demeanor whose effect was like a veil drawn over her sumptuous body. Married to a four-star husband, a chemical engineer from a well-to-do family, with a management post in a multinational firm, Vimla seemed effortlessly to combine modern outlook with traditional values. She ran sophisticated cocktail parties but neither drank nor smoked, socialized in fast company but did not flirt. Vimla played a classical instrument, the veena, went twice a week to sit with her husband's bedridden granny, took driving lessons and tennis lessons, and doted on her two-year-old son. She was a hard act to follow, and from the start, Tanya, two years her junior, opted for a different path.

"Suicide was a big subject in our house last year," Kamla matter-of-factly reported. "Tanya threatened it several times and started fasting. Mummy and Daddy are so opposed to everything she wants to do. She writes very well, and she wants to go for journalism, the crusading kind, exposing scandals and dowry murders. She'd been corresponding with some professional woman journalist who is quite bold. There were awful fights at home, over her privacy, who has the right to open her mail, what she can subscribe to or not. Now that she's twenty-one, she can supposedly do what she likes, but of course it isn't like that. She refuses to hear one word about marriage. When she feels totally trapped she starts her suicides."

"I was getting fed up with her, til one day when Mummy said something outrageous, that showed me what my sister feels up against. She shouted at Tanya that she didn't have any right to commit suicide. It would interfere with *my* marriage! No one would accept a girl from a dishonored family." Kamla paused. "Well, that was a terrible thing, to make my sister feel guilty for spoiling my chances. As if that was the worst thing, worse than her being dead! But Mummy really believed in what she was saying."

It is no wonder that "Mummy" is unprepared for teenage rebellion. Until recent years, there were no acknowledged problems; a girl in her teens was being groomed for betrothal, already metamorphosing into a daughter-in-law. Only in the 1980s were books like *Conflict between Adolescent Girls and Parents in India* written and published here. Like many Bombay mothers, Kamla's was conservative in one domain and flexible in another, prepared to be "open-minded" but inevitably siding with her husband. Kamla herself was of two minds. She felt that Tanya was right to set goals for her own life but wondered if her sister wasn't being too "individualistic." I asked where her brother stood in all this.

Kamla's eyes widened. "He doesn't want to know a thing about it! At the first sign of tension at home, Arjun goes out. His idea of a major problem in life is where to play tennis because we can't afford to join a club."

Until Vimla married and left home, Kamla and Arjun had shared a bedroom and been good pals. Now he was spending most of his time outside. I asked Kamla if having an older brother wasn't an advantage for social life. His circle of friends would be an acceptable group of young men from whom eventually to choose a life partner. Kamla flushed and said she had plenty of time for that! Her mother had married at seventeen but was keen that her girls graduate before they settled down. Home and marriage unquestionably come first, but the modern idea is that a girl should have something to fall back on, in case she finds herself obliged to earn money. As for her brother's friends, they were overgrown brats or painfully shy and much less mature than the girls. "I think there must be a five-year difference in age. My brother-in-law is thirty."

I asked how he and Vimla had met.

"It was arranged! I told you she was Miss Perfect. Vimla

said, 'We don't choose the family we're born into, we adjust to it. So why should we risk choosing our marriage? It's too important to be left up to individual choice.' It was an arrangement by consent. They got to meet each other a few times first. Vijay is related by marriage to my father's cousin. He'd known about Vimla for some time. They were introduced for the purpose of making the match."

I asked Kamla if she knew anyone who had made a love match and what she thought of that.

"In Vimla's college there was a real Romeo and Juliet romance. She was shipped off to boarding school in the middle of term. But you know, I'm not really convinced about romance. We all read romance novels! But love marriages don't seem to work out—look at your country. There's nothing left to bind it together if romance was all they had to start with. Then there's divorce and unhappiness. We have a divorcée in our family now, my mother's eldest brother's daughter. She has a kid, and they live back with her parents."

I asked if this had caused a scandal.

"It must have because it was kept a strict secret from us, the young ones! Lata came home three, four years ago. Everyone said her husband was going abroad for his work. Then the months passed; there were rumors of this and that. And then it seemed there'd been a separation and divorce."

Lata earned her keep by giving private tuition to high school students. Her family had begun prospecting for a new match through the matrimonial columns of *The Times of India*. The text of their notice describes them as "respectable" and "well-placed," their daughter as "innocent divorcée." The copy states that a "well-settled" widower or divorcé might be considered. One cannot be too choosy when putting second-hand goods on the market.

The matrimonial ads in the Sunday papers are fun to read, but they are no joke. Middle- and upper-middle-class families resort to the classifieds to have a wider spectrum of choice. At the end of 1989, *The Hindustan Times*, for one, was listing nearly six thousand matrimonials per month. The terms used in the ads are as easily decoded as real estate rentals in Western papers, where "cozy, full of charm" signifies a tiny, stuffy apartment; "needs sprucing up" signals major costly repairs.

The blue-chip "boy" or "girl" (always so designated, whatever the age) will be handsome and wealthy, the family cultured and well-established (i.e., well-heeled). The girl will in addition be fair-skinned, slim, and tall, convent-educated, and homely—that is, domestically competent and home-loving. A complexion termed "wheatish" is an admission that the maiden is dark; if there is no mention of "beautiful" or "smart," then caveat emptor. Typical advertisements with a certain bona fides, allowing for a standard inflation, are the two below, one for a groom for a Punjabi girl, one for a bride for a Maharashtrian boy, clipped from the Bombay edition of *The Times of India*.

> Alliance for Science Graduate (St. Xavier's, Bombay). Convent-educated Punjabi girl, presently doing Post-graduate Course in Dietetic Science. Twenty-two years, 161 cms. tall, charming, presentable, and having a very friendly nature with a homely disposition. Brought up in a sober, well-connected family. Father with top executive background, now has his own business in Bombay. Desired young man should be well-educated and well-placed, good looking and from a decent, affluent family.
> Reply with Biodata to Box . . . .

> A home loving graduate girl speaking fluent English, having attractive, fair, smart personality, age group 24–28 years from a good cultured respectable Maharashtrian Brahmin, Gujarati or Jain family required for a Maharashtrian Jain boy from a well known cultured family age 32 height 5 feet 6 inches, fair complexioned and handsome personality. Widely travelled. Mechanical engineer M.S. & MBA from USA managing sizeable family business. Advertisement for wider choice. Reply early to Box . . . .

Even in standard announcements of this genre, new trends are discernible that reflect shifts in market values. Teenage marriage is on the wane. Prospective brides are twenty-three, twenty-five, even thirty. Top-value girls are graduates, not totally unfledged nestlings. But more,along with looks and domestic virtues, the proffered or desired girl holds a job. She is a teacher, bank employee, insurance agent, or better still, "medico" (doctor), or government officer, and her salary is indicated. In the Delhi edition of *The Hindustan Times*, a typical abbreviation used to be 22/160, the young woman's age and height. Now there is often a third figure: 22/160/2,200, her monthly earnings. Families of girls with such qualifications can try for higher stakes: a boy who has a green card (U.S. permanent resident) or owns his apartment.

Evolving definitions of status favor certain trade-offs. Particularly in Bombay and Delhi, what receives unctuous lip service may not be what ultimately counts. Executive employment in a multinational firm, computer competency, or access to America can easily compensate for something doubtful in the family name, some obscurity of origin. The criteria have become nakedly materialistic. A young Delhi resident who returned to her native Calcutta when she reached marriageable age was comforted to find the advertisements in the Calcutta *Statesman* less crass. Old-fashioned feminine accomplishments, proficiency in music and dance, or just sheer beauty could still enable an obscure girl to find her match.

Where the facts cannot be masked, families propose and agree to consider divorced or widowed candidates. There are the hope-against-hopers: "Financially strong bachelor amputee willing to accept an understanding poor orphan"; "Recently widowed father of three seeks early alliance with sober good-natured girl, no dowry, caste no bar." It is not rare to find ads placed by divorced or widowed women on their own behalf, without family as intermediary. There is hardly any other way for unattached women discreetly to make themselves known. And nothing, apparently, can be worse for a woman than to remain unattached, a social pariah.

In all the separate and unequal social worlds cohabiting in an Indian city, there is consensus on one point: a woman needs to have married status. At the least, she needs to have had a husband, once. "Mister Right" is not met by chance, and hardly ever is he the boy next door. For a young woman and man to get together through proximity and companionship because they've grown up in neighboring apartments or adjacent tenement rooms is not done. Working-class families settled in Bombay for two generations keep close touch with relatives in the native district, who send out feelers when it comes time to marry off a daughter. Sometimes a match can be found among other families who have migrated from the same region and live elsewhere in the city. Otherwise, a girl born and raised in the Big City may be shipped "home" to marry a village boy.

Against the inevitable social mixing and healthy heterogeneity of urban life, barriers are maintained to assure that certain communities remain intact and certain cultural imperatives are observed. Whomever you may speak to or jostle against in public places, eat next to in a restaurant or school canteen, there are limits to social mixing. The sense of *us* and *them* with its implicit consciousness of one's relative status in the social hierarchy can be blurred, but not blotted out. With practice, as I came to recognize, it can render invisible those others who are not by any reach of the imagination us or ours.

✦ ✦ ✦

One afternoon, Kamla and Vimla offered to take me on a tour of Linking Road, Bandra, the local equivalent of our early suburban shopping malls. Vimla knew the best boutiques for better-than-Italian handbags of native manufacture (but with imported zippers and snaps) and for silk *kurta-pajamas* that would make great evening wear in Paris. At the last minute, the company car and driver that Vimla could commandeer when her husband did not require them, became unavailable. We went out by train. I thought I detected the tiniest suggestion of vexation on Vimla's part, a bit of a pout at having to do without the car. I did not make the error of protesting that I preferred—as in fact I did—the scrimmage of the Western Railway.

Once aboard, Vimla resolved herself into an expression of utter aloofness, as she did when lifting her sari hem to avoid the muck of the street. My attention went to three women who were sitting on the floor, taking up most of the doorway area. Next to them were wide baskets heaped with empty brown coconut shells. They were returning from town with the husks of coconuts they had cracked open and sold by segments. Or else they were simply foragers, who used coconut shells for fuel or sold them to someone who made something out of them, in this society of endless recuperation. Each woman took up three times the space she would have a right to if she'd bought a ticket because each was buttressed with baskets and babies. Every small dirty kid offended in one way or another. One had thick snot hanging from both nostrils; one had a streaky, naked bottom; the heads all looked like lice colonies. To board or leave the train, a little detour had to be made around them. The women didn't pay the least attention. Here, on the rolling floor of the train, in the afternoon breeze, they were enjoying their only time off in an unending day. They laughed, yelled at the children, ate puffed rice from a newsprint packet, rocked back on their haunches. Commuting home from work, like anyone else.

At Mahim Junction, each woman, with a practiced gesture both graceful and economical, scooped a child onto her hip, steadied a coconut basket on her head, and stepped from the moving train—all in one blended and perfectly timed movement, choreography.

When last seen, they were trudging along the tracks, each one a micro-economic unit, to disappear into the maze of kennels where they live, cook food, squabble, laugh, get pushed around by their men, bathe their babies in foul water. Their strong, handsome bodies seemed everything-proof: resistant to germs, filth, hard labor, physical discomfort, abuse. Mother India. Or so we like to imagine.

Once they were gone, there was a perceptible easing of the atmosphere, a closing of the ranks. The rest of us were, after all, women of decent society, and those who were poor and threadbare were at least genteelly so. We left the smell of Mahim behind, occupied the space where they'd been, and prepared for arrival at Bandra.

At the station, Vimla flagged a cycle rickshaw. "I'm so dry," she said. "Let's have him drop us at an Open House for an ice cream soda?"

It would be her treat, of course, and a way of making up for any inconvenience suffered.

"What do those women do with the coconut shells?" I asked.

Kamla shrugged. "No idea."

"Which women?" Vimla asked.

I wondered if Tanya, the rebel in the bud, would have known or cared. But part of Tanya's valiant struggle to position and define herself had been her flat refusal to waste time meeting any well-meaning, note-taking, irrelevant foreigner like me.

• 3 •

THE HAZARDS OF HOMEMAKING

"Great city, terrible place."

—Charles Correa, Bombay architect

Just as the image of the mushroom cloud dominated the consciousness of the second half of this century, the image of the Third World megalopolis, it has been said, will dominate the consciousness of the next. In teeming agglomerations like Bombay, the fallout of the population bomb is that even when people have food, clothes, and money to spend they have nowhere to live.

Bombay, India's boomtown, is in many ways victim of its own dynamic growth. The westward-facing seaport city dates its industrial development back to the advent of cotton mills and railways in the 1850s. With the opening of the Suez Canal in 1869, Bombay's commercial primacy was assured. The ruling British encouraged able businessmen of minority communities, Parsis and Jains, to settle here. Religious liberty and free enterprise thrived together as they had in some of the colonies of British North America. Immigrant populations from the interior were soon attracted to a city where skills, ideas, incentive, and capital had begun to concentrate. Like

New York, Bombay became a city of immigrants and sons of immigrants.

Geographically, Bombay is an appendix on the west coast of India. The peninsula was originally seven separate islands, which have been brought together by reclamation of salt marshes and continuous landfill. Metropolitan Bombay is roughly Y-shaped, expanding linearly north and northeast. The narrow southern end of the city, its historical core and financial heart, is physically saturated. Some older downtown districts have more than 100,000 inhabitants per square mile, and the overall density is nearly four times that of New York. The suburbs have nowhere to go but ever further north and eventually northeast to the mainland. The suburban railways, reaching out thirty-five miles from Churchgate and seventy-five miles from Victoria Terminus, carry five million riders daily. They were designed to transport one-third this number.

Statistics can suggest an order of magnitude; but the human density, the traffic, and the noise have to be experienced. Just waiting for the green walk signal at a downtown intersection, one is engulfed in a crowd the size of the outflow from a stadium exit. The din is constant. Staccato taxi horns (Bombay has forty thousand taxis), braying buses, squawking truck horns, yelping scooters, hawkers whining litanies, handcart pullers hissing their way along, bicycle bells, wailing music from transistor radios—create an almost tangible web of noise. The composite of pavement activity assails the other senses. Along with vendors displaying every conceivable article in gaudy plastic or polyester, there are cut fruit stands, sugarcane juice grinders, coconut heaps, incense fumes, hot snacks roasting and frying, red betel-spit splotches, crows pecking in refuse mounds, and rivulets of gutter sludge. Overlooking it all are the decrepit verandahs hung with clothing, mazes of electric and telephone wire, and the giant billboards displaying garishly colored film personalities, much larger than life.

Along with Calcutta, Bombay was cited by a team of UN experts in 1986 as one of the eight cities most conspicuous for a "wretched, degraded and low quality of life." The team had been studying environmental problems in twenty-two cities of the world. Naming the other six worst offenders makes for a macabre guessing game. But the projections for Bombay alone are horrific enough. The year 2000, that inevitable reference date so close on the horizon, will see Bombay, the world's twelfth-largest city, with a population of fifteen million—roughly equal to the continent of Australia. Ten million of these people will be living in slums.

This might not have the dramatic implications of a mushroom cloud, if a slum resembled what city dwellers in the northern hemisphere know: four walls, a roof and a floor, some plumbing—however insalubrious and grim. In an Indian city, a slum dwelling may be the space underneath a length of gunny sack strung up between two angles of a fence. It may be walls of woven matting propped like a cardhouse or a jumble of improvised kennels that ingeniously recycle industrial waste. A slum may consist of rows of more solid structures of unmortared brick or wallboard or corrugated tin, high enough to stand in, large enough to stretch out in, and tightly enough devised to withstand monsoon rains. But most slums lack electricity, running water, and drainage. Even a communal water tap and latrine block are not always assured. And within each dwelling place live five people, on the average.

Abject poverty is not the exclusive reason why people exist like this. Families with two or three wage earners do have money to spend. One need only count the television antennae sprouting from roofs of shantytowns, where people can afford not only to buy a TV set but also to chip in for a diesel generator to supply the current. But land is so scarce, land prices so steep, speculation and corruption so endemic that, barring a utopian reordering of priorities, there is no way to build the subsidized housing—merely a million two-room units, with infrastructure—that would be within the means of low-income families.

What does the housing nightmare mean for the daily lives of homemakers? The move from rural hut to urban slum makes no difference to the woman, whose chore is still to gather the wood and draw the water. The basic survival tasks always performed by women are only less arduous and time-consuming at higher income levels. Apartment-dwellers cook on burners fed by kerosene or gas cylinders or have kitchens equipped with electric plates. But cooking in the slums is done on an open clay stove (*chulha*) fueled by wood or coal. Wherever there are a few trees standing, it is a common sight to see shantytown women patiently flinging sticks again and again, trying to knock down some dry twigs for a tiny bunch of firewood. Dried cowdung, the staple fuel in the village, is not produced in high-rise neighborhoods.

Morning and evening in the residential streets, women pass with huge brass water pots on their heads. These are not the apartment residents, who have running water, even if it must be boiled and/or filtered for safe drinking. Slum dwellers and pavement squatters carry their daily water from pumps or municipal taps, just as they did in the village. Because of chronic water shortage, these taps may function only from five to eight in the morning and from six to nine in the evening. The predawn lineup of girls and women jostling for position at the taps can be a time for socializing, or it can erupt into fights that serve to release tensions and provide conversation topics for the day.

Those who are correctly housed—which may well mean husband, wife, two children, and a grandparent all in a one-bedroom apartment—are spared the chore of lining up at a street tap. But the higher living standard of the middle-class homemaker is subject to hassles of another order. When the gas runs out, it may take weeks for delivery of a new butane cylinder. Fluctuating electric supply stalls the elevators in residential high-rises; the telephone suddenly goes dead for days. The pressure on municipal services may mean that coming home from the market entails a forty-five minute wait at the bus stop because every bus that passes is too jammed for a woman encumbered by sacks to grapple her way on. The bureaucratic overload guarantees long waits in lines for train tickets, official documents, queries, and application forms. And the diversified, small-scale nature of commerce makes for endless uncombinable errands and unsystematic chores.

The middle-class homemaker can count on an hour or two of daily help from a cleaning woman. She may get an occasional assist from her husband with the shopping or send her children on local errands. But running a household is arduous, especially when combined with an earning activity and conducted in a hot, humid climate where the degree of air pollution—from mills, oil refineries, chemical plants, the diesel engines of 200,000 buses and trucks—is apparent each time you wash your face or pass a hand over a surface that was cleaned a few hours before.

"You get used to it." Not only that: few homemakers show evident signs of wear and tear. In the early morning, the graceful women pass in classic poses, bent arm raised to steady the double water pots balanced on their heads. All are in bright, neatly arranged saris, their glossy hair pulled into a tight chignon, bangles gleaming on their arms. No one looks frumpy or cranky or shows evidence of having already crouched for two hours over her smoky chulha, preparing food on the swept earthen floor of her hut. The apartment-dwelling working mother is in a parallel situation. She is likely to rise before dawn to cook and pack lunches for the whole family before she sets off to work, wearing a neatly ironed sari that can only wilt in the congestion of mass transport.

Of course people complain, but the complaints have a fatalistic ring. Many who bewail the lack of amenities and the deteriorating services are relatively privileged. The apartment they live in may be jerrybuilt, but you get used to that. A standard unit of middle-class housing is likely to be in a drab multistory block, plunked down on a barren plot with a view on a slum. The exterior is streaked and discolored with mold, and the interior shows many signs of shoddy, unskilled work. Floors are not quite level, corners not square, windows are either too loose or stuck tight in their frames. Where paint has been applied, a corolla of gobs and spatters remains. One couple I knew managed to rent a fourth-floor walkup with a good exposure and a bit of sea breeze. But no door hangs quite right; they shudder and bump: tup-wmp, tup-wmp, tup-wmp all day, no matter where the wedges of newspaper are tucked. Do you get used to it?

High-rent payers or apartment owners spend years demanding repairs and taking architects and building contractors to court. But the housing squeeze is so ferocious that what you have you hang onto—even when the walls are filled with carcinogenic fibers or the building's retaining wall is being eaten away by the sea. Or when the apartment complex, correctly built and landscaped, is located in Chembur, the industrial suburb where 50 percent of the city's pollutants are emitted, and the air actually reeks of ammonia.

Real estate scandals are frequent, and revelations, accusations, and endless adjudications are standard items of newspaper fare. But they are not the poignant human dramas. The dramas happen in the middle of the night, when the room you call home simply shears off the backside of the aged tenement and topples into the street below. Or one fine morning when your snug, semipermanent shanty is bulldozed by the municipal demolition squad.

In both cases, citizens have been duly warned. Each year before the monsoon arrives, housing survey teams officially advise tens of thousands of families that their accommodations are in danger of collapse. Countless thousands of others know that they are illegal squatters on government land. But because nobody has anywhere else to go, they stay on, hoping for the best and resigned to face the worst.

It is not always a passive resignation, a mute submission to "fate." Residents' organizations and tenants' associations try to defend their interests and put pressure on authorities.But it is hard to know where to lodge an effective protest or with whom responsibility lies. Take, for example, one century-old, densely-inhabited, five-story dwelling that collapsed in the early hours of March 23, 1986, in the jumbled lanes of the historic Fort section of south Bombay. Among the five dead and twenty injured were many members of the same extended family. The toll would have been higher had the building not been, by chance, very near a fire station. Firefighters arrived within minutes, to pull survivors from the mass of rubble.

A week earlier, residents had complained to their Ward authority about vibrations set off in the building by the reconstruction of a mosque next door. Work on the mosque, which involved digging a deep hole alongside the foundations of the affected structure, had been in progress for some months, but protests by the tenants had gone unheeded. In the legislative council hearing held shortly after the event, no one could say who had given the permission for construction work on the mosque. There is also a question about what authority would have been competent to halt it—a sensitive issue when a religious minority is concerned.

As for the neighbors' complaints, they were no doubt conveyed along a path as winding and obscure as the lanes of the Fort. The protest could have been dismissed at the outset as Hindu residents' interference with the rights of Muslims. Or perhaps it lay as a dead letter at the bottom of a loaded in-basket because no *baksees* (tip) lubricated its upward passage. Perhaps it did land on the desk of some lesser functionary, who sent a memo to another department advising that "steps be taken."

Or, in such a case, it could be that a team of experts is dispatched to inspect the site. The engineer heading the team turns out to be related by marriage to the mosque contractor. The team recommends that sandbags be wedged into the gap between the two buildings. This is duly done, and work recommences.

And so on. One morning or another, the abused and dilapidated structure will crack, walls and floors shear off, and rooms full of people plunge to the ground.

For there are just too many. In 1986, the official list of "cessed" habitations—meaning, those slated to be repaired or rebuilt by the city or state pending acquittal of a tax by the owner—numbered 19,642. In many cases, the owners' lack of maintenance or total abandon was due to frozen rents. The Rent Control Act, in force since the 1940s, has kept the rents of older buildings at absurdly low levels for families who continuously live there, while single family units in new apartment blocks command prices ten or twenty times higher. Neglected by the municipality, maintained by nobody, cessed buildings, in the phrase of a former minister of housing, are like unmarried girls, dependent on their fathers' protection; that is, they are the moral responsibility of the state housing board. The minister affirmed that some 40 million dollars, from various sources, were earmarked for rehabilitation. The press estimated the actual cost of reconstruction or repair of the 19,642 dwellings at twenty-five billion rupees, or 1.5 billion dollars.

And the 600,000 families living there, nearly three million

people? They would have to be relocated for the duration, a period of up to five years in transit camps. Transit camps, which tend to become semipermanent settlements, are in any case already full. One official described it, "As everyone in this city knows, if even two buildings collapse simultaneously, the infrastructure at transit camps collapses with them."

Yet every year, the monsoon season of high winds and torrential rains produces one megacollapse to highlight the situation. Often the victims are the working-class occupants of the industrial tenements known as *chawls:* long, rectangular three-storied rabbit warrens built many decades ago to accommodate textile factory workers and now inhabited by a minimum of one family per room. One such chawl that disintegrated in the August rains left a toll of forty-six killed, fifty-five injured. The building had shown "no signs of distress" during the government inspectors' premonsoon survey. Yet, after the cave-in, the foundation was found to have been weakened by gullies of stagnant water and damaged pipes that created permanent dampness. Illegal workshops and throbbing machinery also took a toll on the already vitiated walls.

In a chawl, each room is a home, and often a worksite as well. The women spend their days indoors or on the sagging verandahs, producing or processing: turning fabric remnants into patchwork covers, stitching simple garments on a treadle sewing machine, cooking meals for mill laborers. Their meager earnings do not simply supplement the family income. They often *are* the family income, when the male head-of-household is unemployed after long months of strikes and shutdowns in the mills.

Chawl dwellers are hard-working, stable families who own radios, even television sets; who decorate their walls with framed photos and colorful calendars; whose children in clean, pressed uniforms go every day to school. Being placed in a transit camp could mean the feared irreversible step backward into the morass of makeshift expedients, in the company of former untouchables and illiterate immigrants from alien regions. The second- or third-generation Bombayite living in a tenement is middle *caste*. This does not imply a level of income or education we would identify as middle *class*, but it means everything in the social context—with regard to how one dresses and eats, one's acquaintance with progressive ideas and access to Western goods, expectations regarding children's education and eventual earning power, and appropriate marriage partners for daughters. From this point of view, unhousement of families of skilled laborers and artisans or low-level white-collar workers can be more traumatic than the eviction of so-called hutment dwellers. The latter can heap their worldly goods on a handcart and head down the road. Their meager possessions are despoiled, the assiduous efforts at housekeeping violated, but their livelihood as vegetable vendors, water distributors, ragpickers, or headload carriers is not endangered. As soon as a colony of squatters is bulldozed, it mushrooms into life in another locale.

In fact, it has become fashionable to point up the positive aspects of this adaptability. Hutment dwellers are tenacious and resourceful. They discern in a cement pipe, a packing crate, a polyvinyl sheet the makings of a habitat. They are demonstrating Darwinian survival, and their few square feet of improvised privacy are not foul kennels, but recognizable human homes.

Such people serve a vital economic function in the surrounding area. They may originally have been recruited as laborers and installed there by contractors for the time it takes to build an office complex or multistory housing block. Once these buildings are delivered, the men of the shantytown may become hawkers or errand-runners. The women take jobs as domestics in the bourgeois apartments. The shantytown begins to function as a community, with a political organization, sometimes aided by activists and social workers from the outside. Yet, when the municipality—often under pressure from neighboring apartment dwellers who don't care for the view—decides that these squatters have to go, the bulldozers can move in without warning.

Such was the case in the spring of 1986. A particularly prime piece of municipal land was urgently required, it was claimed, for a fire station. Although it was true that the clusters of costly new high-rise apartment buildings had no local firehouse, it was also very likely that clearing the land would be the only sign of urgency for some time to come. The *zoppadpatti* (from *zopda,* the Marathi word for *hut*), in any case, was demolished. Forty-eight hours later, a new settlement was in business across the boulevard, about a hundred meters away. The depleted but resurrected structures now sat brazenly right out on the sidewalk. Their ragtag appearance was offset by a show of banners, the Indian flag, the local colors, and those of the political party espoused by the colony. Passengers descending from the bus at that corner would now have to hop-skip along the broken curb, narrowly missing having a leg skinned by a speeding taxi. On the left are garbage piles and slice-of-life views. The feet of a man stretched on his string cot are an inch away. His wife does not look up from slapping chapatis on a flat stone, nor does her little boy move from squatting in situ, placidly defecating while watching the chickens.

Same folks, different venue. This particular group, which had named its movable urban village after the late brother of the then prime minister, was bold with the knowledge of having friends in high places. A support group of film people, lawyers, writers, and social workers had made this colony their cause. They had already courted arrest and much useful publicity through demonstrations. They demanded alternative accommodation and a stay on further demolition . . . at least until school examinations were over. For under these roofs of rags there were said to be three hundred school children, who were studying for end-of-year exams. Some were preparing the secondary school certificate, the only available passport to the kind of white-collar employment that might—*might*—lift them off the pavement.

The tribulations of this colony made front-page news for several weeks. This was unusual: slum demolitions normally don't make much noise. But first, a child from the settlement, an only son, was struck dead, and another child injured, by cars taking the curve of occupied roadside too fast. Then, a celebrated actress joined a handful of hut dwellers (including the woman who cleaned house for the state housing secretary, who lived nearby in a luxury high-rise apartment) to wield the Gandhian weapon, *satyagraha*. An "indefinite" fast was declared. "Indefinite" turned out to last four days, before the publicity and much offstage maneuvering produced official concessions and unspecified promises that ended the hunger strike.

By the fall of 1987, the colony had been transferred to a parcel of land in the suburbs some twenty miles to the north. The new site was in fact a rocky ravine in the process of reclamation. There were no provisions for water or sanitation or for the construction of a school. Unknown was the cost in time and money for the resettled wage earners to commute to their old worksites or if the women who needed work as domestics could find employers nearby. These were not the administration's problems. Land had been found, and the troublesome population dumped on it. The former site was rendered agreeable to look upon, planted with grass and floral borders in contrasting colors.

In a documentary made by a filmmaker involved in the hunger strike, an old woman watches her hut being bulldozed for the fourth time. Wrung dry of hope and past all illusions, she makes the barest request. "All I need is a corner to hide my face." The minimal definition of *home*.

✦ ✦ ✦

Once in a rare while, the grim forces known as fate converge perversely for the good. A Muslim woman, recently widowed, was living on in the once-genteel Bombay residence where she and her late husband had rented rooms. One day, the unpropped rear wall caved in. From the debris, she picked out a notebook which her husband had kept hidden in a crack in the wall. In it she found two items of which she had been totally unaware: his life insurance policy number and the location of a storage shed where he and his brothers had run a small business. Her husband's sister had already filed claim to the insurance, and his brother was taking offers on the storage shed. The widow, who was supporting herself and two small children as a telephone operator, obtained restraining orders against her in-laws and secured the counsel of two women lawyers. The case was judged in the Bombay High Court. The widow stood to obtain two *lakh* rupees (about $12,000) as her rightful inheritance.

Now all she had to do was find a place to live.

◆4◆

CLEANERS AND HANDICRAFTERS

"When I'm not working I'm sleeping."

—Delhi slum woman

Shreemati, who cleaned our apartment every morning, lived in the seaside shantytown that was visible from the upper-story windows of our building. A brackish pond, due to be reclaimed and densely developed, lay between our two settlements. On the morning after the first night of pelting monsoon rain, Shreemati turned up late. She slipped off her plastic sandals at the door and wished us good day. She was wearing her usual blue printed cotton sari in the inelegant but functional Marathi style, pulled up between the legs and tucked at the waist.

We exchanged a word about the weather, and I asked her how her roof was holding. The week before, she had requested an advance on her salary and a morning off to buy and oversee the installation of several meters of bright blue plastic sheeting over the cardboard and woven palm-frond roof of her family's hut. She had to make her home secure before the rains began and the new school year started for her son, the youngest of her five children. "The roof is good," she told me, smiling, "But the floor is wet: water comes in through the doorway. Cooking very difficult," she said matter-of-factly, took up the straw whisk, and went to the bedroom to sweep.

Shreemati had been working for us for several months. Occasionally I, the foreign *memsahib,* would ask her questions about her situation. She would answer fully and at length—when asked. But she never initiated conversation, offered an opinion, or voiced the slightest complaint. Shreemati knew her place. Her reference to the cooking problem was not lost on me. I pictured the creeping water, the sodden earth floor, and the coal fire in the corner smokier than ever, threatening to sputter out.

Shreemati's seventeen-year-old daughter Gouri had cleaned house for us until her marriage three months earlier. We had followed the progress of the marriage preparations, through the increased giggliness of the daughter and the anxiety, then relief of the mother. Shreemati then took over Gouri's work by adding a fifth apartment to the daily four she already "did." She had had to borrow five thousand rupees to make a respectable wedding in their native village. One status-enhancing extravagance had been formal wedding invitations professionally printed in English, for distribution to employers and well-wishers like ourselves.

Like tens of thousands of illiterate working women in Bombay, Shreemati was born and grew up in a village a few hours' bus ride away. Schooling was not available to her. She was married in the 1960s, and her husband decided they would try their luck in the Big City. His brother and his cousin had already migrated and were "settled"—that is, squatting on undeveloped government-owned land at the southern tip of Bombay. The land bordered the huge military reservation where several thousand Navy officers' and enlisted men's families were housed. There was a steady market for shoemaking, the hereditary vocation of the men, and for the one kind of work Shreemati knew, household labor.

She was hired as a domestic in a junior officer's family. Her job was to do everything: cook, wash utensils, launder clothes, scrub the floors, do errands. In return, she had room and board: a mat and blanket on the kitchen floor and a diet of coarse rice, wheat chapatis, and table leftovers. Once in a while, there would be a five-rupee tip or the *largesse* of eighty centimeters of cloth for a new blouse on one of the Hindu holidays when higher status folk give gifts to their inferiors.

The arrangement became difficult after Shreemati had her first child, and with the coming of the second, impossible. She received no money for her work, and payment in kind did not feed her babies. Her husband had not had the initiative to establish his cobbler's trade in the fast-growing high-rise business district of Nariman Point or in the busy shopping streets of Colaba. Others from their shanty settlement had staked out a pavement plot, set up a large black umbrella against sun or rain, and laid out their needles and awls. They'd borrowed or scrounged for the initial investment in shoe polish, synthetic rubber heels, scrap leather, and nails. They were doing business, bringing in twenty-five rupees a day. Not that their wives saw much of it, aside from the few rupees they could wheedle for food rations. Living away from their native village, in refugee-camp conditions, among unfamiliar languages and different religions; subject to the caprices of the cops and petty racketeers, the men suffered what we would term alienation. Many sought solace in country liquor, easy to come by. The slums breed two-legged as well as four-legged predators.

By the time Shreemati had produced a son, after two daughters, she knew she needed to earn money. She became *bai,* the daily who comes to one apartment at eight a.m., to the next at nine-thirty, to X Memsahib at eleven, and to Y Memsahib in the late afternoon. In each apartment, she sweeps the floor with the traditional short-handled brush one has to bend or crouch to use effectively. Then on all fours she swabs the stone-amalgam floors with a damp rag, changing the dirty water in the bucket if you remind her—or if, like Shreemati, she is experienced, conscientious, and eager to please. Then she washes the clothes, and there are always a lot in a hot, humid climate: school uniforms, gym shorts drenched with mud, sweaty undershirts, long petticoats—everything to be got white and clean. She squats or kneels on the cement floor of the washing area, attacking the stains with a stiff brush, beating the garments exactly as her mother had, on a flat stone in the river or by the village pump. After she hangs the washing to dry, she sets about scouring pots and pans under the cold water tap. Her duties may also include pounding spices, ironing, polishing—whatever the memsahib may require.

Four households per day is about the limit, given that before sunrise such women sweep their own huts and cook the day's food for school-going or job-hunting children and for working or idling husbands. At noon, the women go home to eat something and see to the lunch of preschoolers or old folks and perhaps lie down for an hour before the afternoon stint. Shreemati has a good reputation and commands top wages: in 1986, one hundred rupees, today one hundred seventy rupees (ten dollars) per month per household. What else her employers might give—a daily cup of tea, a used sari, a tip at festival time—is *dan,* a gift she may expect, but never suggest.

Women like Shreemati who contrive some kind of work for themselves are referred to as the "unorganized sector" or the "self-employed." They are cleaners, piece-workers, petty producers, traders and vendors, and cottage artisans. They grind and bag spices, roll incense sticks, stitch garments; they turn rag remnants into quilts and waste paper into objects of papier-mâché. They represent 94 percent of nonagricultural employed women in India. These women do gruelling, repetitive work in primitive conditions at derisory pay. They have no wage protection, no organization, little visibility. Some of these occupations, like *zardozi* needlework, demand high concentration and skills passed on from mother to daughter, for generations. Zardozi, the intricate gold and silver embroidery and ornamental stitching on what will be very costly saris and evening wear, is a traditional female occupation in low-income Muslim households so orthodox that the married women rarely set foot outside their own door. Piecework contracts are short-term and brutally ill-paid; materials must be purchased from the same contractor who comes to the door to collect the finished work.

A potentially more organizable activity is rolling *bidis,* those aromatic harsh-burning mini-cigarettes that are chic to smoke in the West. A law passed in 1975 establishes the minimal conditions of employment for India's five million bidimakers. But 90 percent of them are home-based women, who have rarely been able to benefit. Mothers, daughters, and neighbors sit in their room or on their common verandah filling, rolling, and tying bidis at impressively rapid rates. They must: earnings are a few rupees per thousand bidis. In 1982, the legal minimum wage was eleven rupees per thousand, but workers were paid far less; many women workers received barely four rupees. By 1988, women who had become unionized were earning thirteen rupees per thousand, although the legal minimum wage by then was seventeen rupees. Not only are men's rates often higher for the same manual task, but men, working in a factory setting, are also eligible for bonuses and welfare benefits. But when male workers organize to demand fairer rates, bidi manufacturers prefer to close the workplace and farm out contracts to cheaper female labor.

Undeniably, men in such occupations are also exploited, underpaid, and subject to unhygienic conditions. But in India's expanding economy, men in low-status jobs have a chance to move up, through group mobilization or individual initiative. The case of the sweepers is illustrative. Sweeper means doer of dirty work, like cleaning public latrines and carting garbage. In the Indian context, the work is done by former untouchables, the lowest of the low on the social scale. In New Delhi it has become the sinecure of a particular caste, the Balmikis. Employed by the municipality or public corporations, the men are unionized and receive low but negotiable wages, bonuses, and minimum benefits such as sick leave. Their wives and daughters, in the unorganized sector, clean private homes and offices or scavenge salable rubbish in the streets. An ambitious and upwardly mobile Balmiki man has a chance to "pass" by wearing Western attire, learning a skill or trade, even adopting a less readily identified family name. During this transitional time, his womenfolk continue the standard, menial jobs that support the family. The wives facilitate the men's social advancement and rapidly find themselves wanting. Here is my man, a woman will think, doing so well, while I am only good for low, dirty work—not fit for so fine a man's wife.

Once he has stabilized his economic position, the husband

may wish to consolidate the rise in family status by retiring his wife from outside labor. She may be more than willing to remain indoors and attend to household duties. She hasn't much choice because no remunerative employment is appropriate for her. Former untouchables, now dubbed "scheduled castes," are eligible for preferential treatment in some domains. But few scheduled caste women of Shreemati's generation can read or write. Housecleaning is the one work they can do for which there will always be a demand. The climate and the economic situation assure it: the high level of air pollution and dust, short preservability of foodstuffs, the absence of labor-saving devices and paper disposables. Should a high-minded middle-class family attempt to do all the home maintenance and childcare tasks without the services of maids, sweepers, and errand-runners, they would have little time to accomplish anything else.

Even families on the lower fringe of the middle class manage to afford some daily domestic help. The haggling between a homemaker whose husband doles out a monthly allowance insufficient for the needs of a six-member family in a two-and-a-half-room apartment, and her *bai,* whose home is a rusty sheet-metal shed and whose son needs medical care, over a monthly wage increase of ten rupees (about sixty cents) is pitiful and edifying. But in the last analysis, a maid can always be dismissed. And no matter how domineering or mean-spirited an employer may be, she is sure to be able to find someone else who needs the work.

In Bombay, most high-rise apartment complexes are skirted by shanty colonies. The maids come and go, jaunty teenagers to toughened grandmothers. Many are balancing heavy brass water jars on their heads. Access to running water, which they tote home twice a day, can be an unofficial perquisite of their work.

Some employers take a personal interest in the welfare of their maidservant and her children. Still, "lazy," "unreliable," "never keeps timings" are staple conversational bits of the memsahibs, many of whom have jobs and fixed schedules of their own. "Chicken is so expensive"; "butcher weighs too many bones in with the mutton"; "my maid didn't turn up, *again.*" It's such a standard tale that a newspaper advertisement introducing the squeeze-sponge floor mop—a piece of intermediate technology designed for the "modern woman" to operate herself—relies upon the following message of complicity with the target housewife.

> I took a SuperMop home [says a pretty, smiling face] and my husband said, "Phazool Kharch" [money down the drain]. Now he's changed his mind. No more jhaddus [broom whisks], no more swabs. No more dependence on the lazy, ever late maid. Just squeeze and sweep . . .

A while ago, in one residence where Shreemati works, someone decided that there was too much exploitation. The pay rate was unrealistic for the amount of work and time expected, given the high cost of living in Bombay. The woman who concluded that it was time for the maids to make a stand was from the Other Side—a young married doctoral student and active feminist. Roused by various atrocities committed against women elsewhere in the city, she had helped organize protest marches, form delegations, and distribute tracts. Now close to home she saw a chronic injustice to take up.

Sujata went down to the shanties and talked to the maids. A few days later, the maids entered the compound in a body and sat outside on the steps. No one went to work. "All very well for her," the homemakers complained. "Sujata is a radical, she lives in one room, she takes all her meals in a canteen, she has no children. Let her live the way she wants. But we have husbands to feed, classes to teach, diapers to be boiled."

Again the next day, the maids sat on the stairs. They said they wanted to talk money, hours, mutual obligations. What they wanted amounted to job descriptions and commensurate pay. For their strike to be taken seriously, it was crucial that no individual housemaid negotiate separately with her employers. But perceiving and asserting a common class interest, rather than bow to traditional allegiances, were not so evident, especially for the older women. These long-time housemaids were loyal to a memsahib who had always helped out when there was a medical emergency, who was generous with children's school supplies, who had arranged for math tutoring for the slum family's first tenth-grade graduate, and who could be relied upon for small loans, advice, kindness.

It is not easy to challenge such habits of devotion and self-denial. The less militant protesters were no doubt relieved when, on the third day of the strike, one of the most fair-minded and respected of the homemakers came forward to propose herself as negotiator.

The maids' *morcha* (protest demonstration) would not have taken place were it not for an outside instigator (who was, however, not a stranger) and the fact that the women all worked in one mini-community, rather than in isolated homes. Its outcome was not spectacular. Wages improved a bit, but no spark of shared sisterhood was kindled between the memsahibs and the maids. Rather, whatever sympathy developed for the maids resulted from a new appreciation of their domestic problems, and these were seen as functions of their lower-class status. For instance, the homemakers learned that many of these women were the sole, or sole reliable, contributor to their family's income.

It is commonly believed—and not only in India—that men have a right to strike for decent pay because they have families to support, while women, who are "self-employed" can afford to work for less. This is doubly erroneous in the lower sectors of Indian society. The first misconception is that women are primarily housewives who occasionally participate in the labor market. The second resides in the term "self-employed," implying ownership or control of the means and conditions of her employment. This is rarely the case. The self-employed woman is neither working for herself nor spending her earnings on herself. Working to maintain the family, she puts her earnings into family subsistence, while the man generally keeps back some part of his. A female worker in the unorganized sector has a good chance of having a husband who is out of work, irregularly employed, or simply no'count. A survey done in 1988 in Ahmedabad, of four hundred women who make their living grinding chilis and spices, found that nearly one-fourth had unemployed husbands, more than one-third were solely dependent on their own income, and more than one-half did not know how much their husbands earned. And many have no husband at all. Analysis of the 1971 census figures in the three southern states of Andhra Pradesh, Karnataka, and Kerala showed that between 12 and 17 percent of households were headed by deserted, divorced, or widowed women. More recent, smaller-scale studies indicate a much higher figure, which would be consistent with both the emigration of male workers to industrial Indian cities or oil-rich Gulf states and the rising rates of desertion and divorce.

But subtler and more tenacious than the misnomer, self-employed, is the confusion about the actual nature of women's productive work. In the family hut or compound, it is difficult to differentiate between domestic chores, contribution to subsistence needs, and cash-earning activity. Where home is also the workplace, income-generating occupations like grinding and bagging spices, tending hens for eggs, or weaving baskets, overlap with housework and seem only extensions of the three C's—cooking, cleaning, and childcare. Nowhere more than in India is the truth of the old saw so evident: women's work is *never* done.

In 1987, the first national Commission on Self-Employed Women was appointed to document the condition of female workers of the informal sector and recommend ways of organizing and improving the status of these workers. Long overdue, this was the first official recognition of the productive labor of millions of women. The report, submitted to the prime minister in 1988, received considerable attention; to date, however, no major policy initiatives have emerged.

Whatever the concrete benefits might eventually be, they will not change anything for Shreemati's generation. Nor is Gouri likely to turn them to her advantage. Gouri has attended school too irregularly to learn much. Her father saw no point in her going, and neither did she. Pert and quick-witted, she knows the words of dozens of Hindi film songs. She croons them as she squats to wash clothes. Gouri's marriage did not suit her. The young man was making a steady living back in the village, but village life won't do for a Bombay girl. A few months after the wedding, she reappeared in her mother's hut and took up the old work—demeaning work, to my eyes. I assumed it was a comedown for her to be separated from her husband and back to duckwalking along the floor, swabbing under people's half-lifted feet.

Gouri does not see it that way. Being married gives her status—frees her from head-wagging and social pressure. She hasn't definitively quit her husband, of course: at seventeen, she is keeping her options open. Back in town, under her mother's roof, she can work as many hours as she needs to earn her keep and have money for cosmetics or the cinema. She values the fact that she has ready access to fine apartments and higher society.

Mother and daughter now turn up as a housework team. Shreemati is as always efficient and discreet. Gouri prefers to flip on the radio while she works. She manages to show herself often at the window, putting her head out to make disobliging remarks to lesser beings down below, the hawkers and headload carriers who can never dream of passing the threshhold.

✦ 5 ✦

FETCHERS AND CARRIERS

Sometimes, at the end of the working day, I would station myself a little distance from the exit gates, to witness the scene. Six o'clock was quitting time for the labor crews who were constructing, literally by hand, multistory extensions of the research institute. Within these walls sat mathematicians thinking about vector bundles and physicists calculating the inflation of the universe on the latest Mainframe VAX.

The laborers were young migrant couples from parched villages in backward areas of Maharashtra and its neighboring states. Husbands and wives worked on the site, with small children keeping an eye on smaller children nearby. There were no hard hats, no cranes, no machinery—just bamboo scaffolding, ropes and pulleys, strong backs, and many, many hands.

From the left gate of the campus the laborers came streaming. Many women were in multilayered gypsylike gear. They wore long flounced skirts and open-backed bodices hung with biblike pieces that glimmered with gilt thread, embroidered patches, and mirror work. Violet and fuschia, scarlet and orange, bold floral pattern on bolder—the whole made a marvelous regalia, resplendent as a macaw's plumage.

Just as vivid were the smiling faces and the proud and jaunty bearing. Families came trooping out together, the young father in *lungi* (a type of sarong), carrying the baby, who wriggled and stared with *kohl*-rimmed eyes; the young mother holding the older child by the hand. Chattering away, they looked as if they were off to a picnic.

From the right-hand gate issued the men and women who worked *inside* the institute—scientists, administrators, secretaries, accountants. They weren't much to look at, in polyester shirts and trousers, sober-toned saris. An office crowd, a bit rumpled and stoop-shouldered, abstracted of eye, fatigued of brow, and drab as pigeons.

Appearances don't really deceive: everyone knows which is the more propitious gate. But an uninstructed eye could momentarily doubt.

The work goes on from nine to six, six days a week. The women pound rock into gravel with small mallets or transport lengths of iron pipe on their heads, by pairs. Their main work is to carry headloads. Moving at a slow, swaying pace, they balance the basketfuls of cement and mortar to wherever they are needed. The men climb about in the scaffolding, caulking, scraping, and chipping, half-naked in shorts or loincloth and grimy head-rag. The women, whose attire and modesty preclude such activity, work on the ground or on top of the story just finished. The work is antlike and unvarying, the daily increment not easy to see.

Road crews who lay pipes or make urgent repairs proceed at a more noticeable pace. For several weeks, my daily bus detoured around the gaping trenches and rubbish hillocks of a road excavation site. To one side stood heaps of rough-cast bricks. One morning, I watched a human chain handing the bricks, exactly like a village bucket brigade in the eighteenth century of the West. A man picked up a brick in each hand, passed them to a woman, she to another, and on to another. At the end of the line, the bricks were restacked, ready for whatever use. In the ninety-degree heat the laborers reached, took, handed off, for hours, keeping a steady rhythm, letting no brick drop.

Was this the ancient, time-honored method? Not necessarily. Back in 2000 B.C.E., the meticulously planned city of Mohenjo-Daro was constructed all of brick. This first urban civilization on the Indus River had drainage canals, ventilation ducts, and water closets. Its artisans might well have employed an advanced technology, the wooden wheelbarrow. But on this Bombay roadsite, a few years short of 2000 C.E., the wheel had not yet been invented.

Making a quick count of the brick-handlers and headloaders, everyone whose sole job was to lift and carry, I recognized that bringing in a wheelbarrow would make several workers redundant. Even with a generous deployment of hands—three people to load, two to push, one to go alongside to steady the barrow—each full trundled barrow would replace several pairs of hands. But the contractor's aim, I supposed, was to get the job done at a profit, not to create employment. Wheelbarrows would be a minimal investment for him, and this sturdy implement would save on wages. But so long as no other contractor's crew has made itself more competitive through such an innovation, the incentive is lacking. And raw, redundant, human labor is still dirt cheap.

Furthermore, to introduce a tool would cause perturbations: division of the labor along gender lines. Manipulating the barrow would become the prerogative of the men. Just as it is in the fields, women weed, transplant, and winnow—the back-bending manual toil. The plow with its prestige is exclusively for the men. Women do not handle tools because they are considered inferior workers or just inherently inferior. Brahmanic orthodoxy reinforces this by teaching that a woman's hand on plow or tractor causes ritual pollution and can jeopardize the harvest. The road-diggers still live in the hierarchically ordered world of their fathers. They accept the constraints their inferior status imposes. And the men cling fast to their male prerogatives, against any unlikely challenge that might come from the women of their community.

The appearance of a labor-saving tool could prove disruptive. Instead of the foreman simply confiding so many thousands of bricks to so many pairs of hands, agreements would have to be reached. Who loads, who unloads, and what is the relative worth of each differentiated activity? The men would control the barrows; efficiency would increase—and the first workers to be laid off would be women. This simple instance of "technological exclusion" is happening at all levels of the Indian economy.

Wherever the introduction of a new technique or skilled operation raises the yield per unit of labor time, the job thence becomes a male job with a higher wage. Obviously, the modernization of India requires greatly enhanced productivity and efficiency and involves a huge investment in technology and skills training. Because a woman is assumed to be *by nature* not apt for the more demanding work and *by function* a homebody with no firm commitment to the labor force, she has little access to these opportunities. Sectors that traditionally employed women—the old-fashioned textile mills, the food-processing and pharmaceuticals industries—are either in decline or are replacing mechanical procedures and manual assembly lines with automated equipment. While redundant male workers have some chance of being absorbed elsewhere, women are just let go. Thus, the semiskilled, poorly educated woman has no choice but to fall back on the marginal occupations compatible with her family or community traditions—vending produce, trading articles, doing piecework at home. She is back in the unorganized sector, where, despite her real economic contribution, she has no recognized status or legal protection.

Even where protective legislation does exist, the laws are the meekest of paper tigers. Construction workers are in principle covered by such laws. The Equal Remuneration Act of 1976 requires employers to pay equal wages to men and women for the same or similar work and not to discriminate on grounds of sex at the time of recruitment. Yet everyone knows and accepts several differential wage scales. In Bombay, where wages are high, the official pay (in 1990) is twenty-five rupees a day for male construction workers, twenty-two for female. Only experienced, unionized crews can command such rates. Fresh recruits from the villages, brought in by labor subcontractors, will earn a maximum of twenty-two rupees per day for the men, seventeen for the women. Work sites are rarely inspected, and the Equal Remuneration Act is hardly every enforced; most laborers have never even heard of it. (A survey made in 1986 in another fast-developing state found that more than 90 percent of the unskilled laborers had no idea that any such law existed.) Nor would it do them much good if they knew. Cheating and exploitation, especially of women, are systematic. Paymasters may take the worker's sign or thumb print on blank paper and fill in the wage figures later. Deferred pay and unexplained fines are common. Any complaint can lead to dismissal.

But who is likely to complain? Here is a population whose

conditions of life are close to those of indentured laborers. They have no notion of rights, no language for seeking redress, and no information about how to do so. The large proportion that speaks in local dialects is not at home in the languages of Bombay. The laborers know their own *mukkadam* (labor recruiter) and fellow villagers, greenhorns like themselves. They do not know the name of their employer; only that he leases them a ten-square-foot hut to live in and can be counted on for several years' steady work and steady pay—provided no one is injured or falls sick. And the wages are far higher than any they have known. Back in their home villages, women laboring the land have to make do with three or four rupees a day.

Their activity begins as soon as the earth-moving machinery and pile drivers have prepared the foundations for the apartment complex, office tower, or commercial center destined for Bombay's solid citizens—the Other Half. For months, the work goes on in mud and slush. Young women, steadying a basketful of cement on their heads with one hand and supporting a clinging baby with the other, climb slippery grades or teeter across planks bridging deep ditches of stagnant water. Toddlers may wander nearby. The young mothers prefer to keep them in sight, rather than leave them back at the huts under the distracted eye of an older child or untrustworthy neighbor.

None of this is necessary or legal. The Contract Labour Act of 1970 requires builders to provide a day-care facility wherever twenty or more women are employed. The utter impunity with which this law is flouted is only one of many scandals surrounding the construction industry, notorious for profiteering and corruption. The day-care facility requirement is merely that: the builder is to provide solid shedlike structures at a safe distance from the building in progress. The care—basic hygiene, nutritious noon meal, supervised play, learning activities leading to school readiness—are the province of social service agencies. For nearly twenty years, Mobile Creches has been struggling to provide such services. At any given time, this organization is operating twenty or so on-site day-care centers in Bombay and Delhi. Yet fewer than 10 percent of ongoing construction sites are served. Builders have been reluctant to commit space and facilities and to contribute to the running costs. Those who do so tend to be in public-sector projects, financed by the central government or the municipality, and located in showcase areas downtown, rather than away in the suburbs, out of sight and mind.

But recalcitrant builders and bribable officials are not the only obstacles to delivering day care. Initial resistance—either passive indifference or open hostility—often comes from the target group itself. The women particularly live in a narrow and archaic mental universe. Married at fifteen or sixteen, most of them give birth in the hut. Pregnancies are frequent because they do not know how to prevent them. Some women do consider sterilization, but they fear that their husbands will thence reject them and worry that the operation may permanently sap their physical strength. Moreover, the child mortality rate is very high. Ritual taboos, such as that against colostrum, are observed; by abstaining from nursing until the third or fourth day after delivery, they deprive the newborns of natural immunities.

Wary of social workers, these women also take a dim view of initiatives shown by any of their peers. Lakshmibai, a veteran construction worker in her early thirties, was trained as an auxiliary health worker. But her interventions merely put her neighbors on the defensive. "Who are you to tell us?" And when asked to encourage other mothers to send their children to the creche as she did, Lakshmibai had no confidence in her own authority. "Who am I to tell them?" she wanted to know.

No direct pressure can be put on these women to send their children to creche or school. They do not see the good of it: they are merely transient, moving from site to site and never at home. Unlike the tenacious sidewalk squatters and slum-dwellers, who place their hopes in the city that has become their children's real home, the migrant laborers neither plan for the future nor imagine how their children could live any differently from themselves. At any time, 50 percent of the preschool and school-age children are wandering about on their own.

Yet the creche, rudimentary and overcrowded as it is, is a hopeful place. In one large cubicle, a ceiling fan hanging from the corrugated metal roof stirs the sultry air over the babies napping. There is no place to set one's foot: the floor is literally carpeted with babies. Tiny wrinkled feet of wailing newborns poke out from rows of cotton slings ingeniously hung from parallel bars fixed to the wall. In the next room, two- and three-year-olds are sitting in groups listening to a creche worker tell a story, holding up bright, simple pictures of birds and animals. Next door, the kindergarten-age children are learning a song, putting up their fingers to show the numbers, one, two, three.

At the end of the day, they join their parents and go home. Proudly, they tell something they have learned or demonstrate what they can do. Sometimes a parent pays attention and makes a connection. Through the young children, simple information about hygiene, nutrition, and resource management filters back to the home; sometimes, it makes an impact.

But nothing may happen. Like a magnetic field where all arrows converge, many positive factors must operate simultaneously: a construction site with an adequate creche facility; a lengthy enough building project to assure that families stay put for two or three years; timely interventions on the part of health and welfare services, for vaccination and basic maternal and child health care; patient efforts of social workers and activists to help workers obtain ration cards, which not only give access to subsidized foodstuffs but also confer on the bearer legitimacy and a sense of belonging. With similar assistance, birth certificates can be established for the children so they can be enrolled in municipal schools; and evening literacy classes set up for adults.

Rare is the construction site where all these factors converge. Such a thing would not be in anyone's interest. Not the builder, who wants the maximum of work and the minimum of bother. Not the middle-class families who have put down a million rupees and then waited, for years, to see their apartments materialize. Not the municipality, lacking an urbanization policy and accumulating debt (as of January 1988 3.24 billion rupees or $191 million).

Eventually, this subproletariat moves on. With luck, the same workers will find themselves regrouped on a new construction site not too far away. Still marginal, they are now more cohesive and citywise. In just a year or two of living in Bombay, these country cousins have had to make more mental adjustments than their forebears did over decades, or even centuries. Much that seemed immutably ordained back in the ancestral village is actually highly subject to circumstance. And no longer is there an authoritative father or mother-in-law in the household to make the decisions and lay down the law.

The men and the adolescent boys rapidly spot the possibilities that exist even for those at the bottom of the heap. They find ways to earn a few extra rupees to spend on gadgets or the collective rental of a TV. For the mothers, wives, and daughters, the exposure to the city is more limited and likely to be more baffling. Job and household duties confine them to the worksite/homesite. And cultural factors block their access to the skills and resources available to the men.

Furthermore, the menfolk and the women, too, know that it is incumbent on women to respect and maintain the traditions of the past—whatever is left of a heritage now vitiated by generations of poverty and ignorance. Women brick-loaders, stone-breakers, and headload carriers, who are first-generation urban migrants, may well show a self-protective lack of curiosity and resist acquiring new knowledge or competencies. For them, being the tradition-bearer virtually means being the one who does not change: does not absorb new impressions, experience new needs, or voice new demands. Yet this desideratum is at odds with the predominant culture of the city itself, brash with acquisition, consumption, and display. The challenge for these women, no less than for the comfortable cosmopolites in their brand-new apartments, is how to evolve an outlook more consistent with modern city survival—without losing, or at least without seeming to lose, anything of their essential "Indianness."

✦ 6 ✦

INGREDIENTS OF EVERYDAY LIFE

. . . winged, unmiraculous women,
Honey-drudgers.

—Sylvia Plath, "Stings"

GITA AND ANITA

Driving home from a concert one sweltering evening, Gita and I got talking about spinach. Gita is a strict vegetarian who often prepares two full meals a day for her family: rice, lentils, spiced cooked greens, a mixed vegetable curry, home-made yoghurt, chutney, a sweet. She is a polyvalent person who has, not one full-time job with office and co-workers, but several part-time activities she pursues from home. She is a professional translator, correspondent for a women's magazine, and occasional producer for All-India Radio of cultural programs for which she travels all over the country.

Gita has a certain heritage. Her mother married at fifteen and bore and raised several children. Then she earned bachelor's and master's degrees and now teaches in a college. Her grandmother, who is in her eighties, can recall the years when, at the "polluted" time of month, she was kept apart in a special room, away from the kitchen and any contact with the family's food. She had looked forward to those days, not just for the respite in household work. She devoted this time to copying out from tattered and fading music sheets the *ragas* that her father sang.

Gita and I were bemoaning the poor quality of vegetables in the neighborhood market. For her, there were few alternatives. I had several, like farm-fresh chicken, cut to order at the meat store that reeked of carrion. A Goan Christian woman ruled the establishment, while her "boys," young men of low-caste origins, handled the dirty work. Here, one could purchase cured Yorkshire-style ham, cheddar cheese from the Ootacamund Hills, and ground mutton burgers. There was even a species of steak—slabs of hacked buffalo-cow flesh—that I'd slice fine and drown in soy sauce.

Gita, who is fluent in four languages, was describing the particular intransigence of spinach—not the dark green, broad-leaved vegetable I knew, but a variety of leaf closer to the size of watercress. Untidy bunches, stems pointing every which way, are heaped in a newspaper parcel along with roots, flowering buds, insects, inedible grasses, and dirt. A kilo is an armful to sort through, each leaf to be stripped individually, all of them to be washed in two waters, drained, spread to dry, and eventually chopped. Gita does it, but with ill grace, watching the clock and not the least serene. She does not consider cleaning spinach to be part of her mission on earth.

I borrowed Tillie Olsen's *Silences* from the U.S. Information Service library to read to Gita from the notebook of Anna Tsetsaeyva.

> It is my notebook that keeps me above the surface of the waters. . . . I've been driven so hard by life that I feel nothing. Through these years it was not my mind that grew numb, but my soul. An astonishing observation: it is precisely for feeling that one needs time, and not for thought. . . . A basic example: rolling 1½ kg of small fishes in flour, I am able to think, but as for feeling—no. The smell is in the way. The smell is in the way, my sticky hands are in the way, the squirting oil in the way, *the fish* are in the way, each one individually and the entire 1½ kg as a whole.

Spinach was very much in Gita's way. She resented preparing it; she persisted in preparing it; she grousedF. Other women we knew confronted the daily food-processing marathon in a resigned and cheerful spirit, as did Priya, or found shortcuts and alternatives. Padma's husband took care of the heavy shopping. Anita had a small freezer chest and an electric mixer. Provided there was no untimely power cut, she could have dinner on the table less than an hour after she got home from work.

The two-way stretch—"I must carry out what is traditional and ineluctable, but I *will* do what satisfies and expresses *me*"—is epitomized in Gita. If her elder son has to be at soccer practice at six a.m., Gita will get up at five to wake him and prepare his breakfast. If her husband and children want to watch the tennis championships on their color TV, Gita, who has an article due, will sit cross-legged on the bedroom floor before her Smith-Corona manual, composing her fifteen hundred words on food adulteration or child labor while the crowds roar through the wall, direct by satellite from Forest Hills.

Ten years ago, when Gita first began to write and send out her work, she had no expectations of either acceptance (which was nearly immediate) or recognition at home. Her children were still young, and her husband had his own demanding work. No one expected him to adjust in his way of living; it was enough if he didn't throw in a monkey wrench.

A "cooperative attitude," according to a group of married women university students interviewed at that time,[1] means that the husband creates a "pleasant atmosphere." He doesn't stand in the way of their studying, if they can fit it in. The women expect to have to fulfill a triple role. Continuing studies is a self-indulgence; extra burdens are the logical result. In Gita's mother's time, generally a servant or dependent female relative was in the house to pick up the burden. In today's urban nuclear family, the whole responsibility is likely to fall on the homemaker alone.

Gita had been hesitant, feeling quite guilty about her need to look for satisfaction outside the domestic sphere. As her competence grew—she writes gracefully in her vernacular and in English—and the demand and the remuneration both increased, it was not her self-confidence that kept pace, but her determination and a sense of the legitimacy of certain expectations. Why shouldn't husband and children acknowledge her professional activity in a tangible way? Surely they could lend a helping hand, or at least lower the demands a notch or two. Preparing for an assignment, Gita loses hours waiting in lines for train tickets and photocopies. But she won't leave town without cooking enough food to cover her absence. At the same time that she believes she has a right to expect some cooperation, she fatalistically accepts not getting any. She goes on managing everything, feeling run-down and fed-up, to the point of confiding personal details to a friend—something not so commonly done in Gita's milieu as it is among women in the West.

Women of Gita's class are sociable and obliging, but not often on intimate terms with one another. To seek friends outside the network of sisters-in-law, cousins, and old family connections is a relatively new phenomenon, accompanying the breakup of the joint family and life in heterogeneous apartment blocks. Mature friendships based on recognition of affinities imply a greater investment than the stereotyped social arrangements dictated by family standing. Young married women have dispensed with some Victorian formalities of their elders, but not with the constraints. They consider it a breach of manners and betrayal of the sanctity of the home to make remarks about their husbands. Rare is the woman who pronounces her husband's first name in conversation: the respectful custom is to refer to him as My Husband, or He.

In general, a middle-class Indian woman does not "let it all hang out." In groups whose bond is a common mother tongue, the women relax and chatter, often going off into giggles like the schoolgirls they seem to re-become. A cluster of dark-haired women in bright saris picnicking on a spread blanket gives an impression of something Victorian and virginal. There is no lack of talk, but much of it is chitchat.

This does not mean that women never get down to brass tacks. But their brass tacks are different. Friends exchange gripes about their mothers-in-law and other mixed blessings in their lives. But almost certainly sex is a topic not to be raised. A high percentage of educated women never had sexual matters adequately explained to them before marriage; according to some sociologists, the figure is over 60 percent.[2] Indian women researchers frequently mention the reluctance of their middle-class interviewees to answer—even to listen to—direct questions about sex. These respondents claim they never discuss sex-related topics with their friends. Menstruation, intercourse, childbirth are "natural" and "inevitable" phenomena; but like personal hygiene, they are not the sort of things you talk about.

What then about intimacy in their married lives? A Frenchwoman visiting Bombay once took me aside to demand, "What are their marriages *like*?" She had observed how, in contrast to the unabashed affection lavished on just about any small child, signs of special regard between men and women were rare and discreetly veiled. "Even with educated people who have seen something of the world," she commented, "at parties, women sit and men stand in separate circles. Wives don't talk to their husbands, and never to other women's husbands. In the street I never see a man and woman walking hand in hand or arm in arm. With married people, I sense a reserve: two separate spheres. Where is the complicity, the current? Do they ever do anything kooky? Do they have any fun?"

Once, for a magazine inquiry, Gita gathered a group of acquaintances in their thirties and forties, to talk about what they wanted and expected from marriage. Sexual fulfillment and sexual compatability were not mentioned. Even a touch of romance, of *courtoisie,* did not make the list. The women spoke of the need for "peace and harmony in marriage," "a peaceful life." Passion, novelty—vital ingredients in marriage recipes in women's magazines in the West—were not cited. But the women did speak up about the lack of appreciation of their worth as individuals. They would have liked their husbands to provide more companionship and help in the home. It was a question of a more democratic distribution of rights and duties, in a partnership geared to founding a household and raising progeny. The nature and viability of the enterprise were not at issue, only some of the modi operandi.

Perhaps because they knew each other socially, these women were a little inhibited in their expression. For some, just to take part in such a discussion must have been a bold move. The emphasis on body consciousness and sexual gratification is in any case widely considered a Western preoccupation that does not fit with Indian options and lifestyles. A workshop of feminist health professionals and activists summed up their own attitudes toward exploring sexuality:

> While all . . . present agreed that a woman has a right to control her own body and to enjoy sex, it was obvious that most of us have not resolved this problem in our own lives. This has partly to do with the fact that consciousness grew during a married life which had been started under more traditional assumptions. Even feminists find acceptance of sexual rights of single women at times difficult. Another factor seemed to be that many of us do not give sex a very high priority in our lives. Most of us did not seem to have sex very frequently or be very dependent on it for emotional gratification. Our priorities are freedom of movement, equitable division of labor, getting our work done, advancing the women's movement, coping with children. [3]

This is a full enough agenda, and it is neither exhaustive nor exclusively a concern of feminists. My neighbor Anita was one of the group whom Gita interviewed for her magazine piece. At the time, Anita was trying to organize her life and her household more efficiently. Her two daughters were in their teens, and she had landed a part-time job. Anita looks the very model of the "new woman," the middle-class consumer who is the prime target of billboard, newspaper, and television advertising. Poised and efficient, mature but not matronly, her well-cut hair worn loose around her face, Anita is informed and independent, at least regarding her buying power. When I learned she was going to work in an advertising agency, I called her attention to some full-page newspaper ads I found offensive. The product was an expensive novelty, a dishwashing liquid in a plastic dispenser. The pitch was condescending in the extreme, baldly flattering "today's woman, the new woman," "who knows what to do with her graduation certificate." Purchase X liquid concentrate: "It's come because you've arrived."

Anita scoffed at the tactic. "Who is going to buy it?" she asked. "Women who don't have a maid to do the washing-up haven't the money for this. And women who do aren't going to squander money on luxuries for the maid!" Yet it was Anita who, one morning, suddenly felt irritated by the sight of her own maid swabbing the floor on all fours. Whether it was the indignity of the method, or its inefficiency, or just an aesthetic aversion, Anita found herself asking, "Why does this woman have to do like this?" She went to have a look at the squeeze-sponge mops on promotion at Akbarally's, an upmarket department store. Knowing that her husband might veto the expense, Anita decided first to sound out her maid. The publicity folder she brought home showed a woman like herself, gracefully wielding the mop. The maid could not make the connection. Suddenly memsahib was not satisfied with her? With a new set of scrub cloths, she could give a better result. And by the way, could she take home the old ones? As for walking around pushing a stick—*Kai hé!* Which is as good as "No way" in Marathi.

Later, we heard the maids in the stairwell laughing over the outlandish proposal. Anita let the matter drop. She has weightier issues to face, which no woman in her family has had to face before. Her widowed mother lives alone in the old family home in the south, looked after by a servant couple, faithful retainers from a simpler past. The old man has cataracts, and the couple want to be pensioned off and retire to their native village. It is not clear what to do. Anita's mother refuses to go live with her son in Canada. To hire new servants is risky: they are untrustworthy, disrespectful, and expensive. Besides, there is the question of companionship and daughterly duty. But there are only two bedrooms in Anita's apartment. Anita's sister already lives with her mother-in-law; in fact, she is the daughter-in-law in her husband's mother's home. She has three sons, and no daughter to share her duties. Yet, as Anita knows, one can no longer tell about daughters. Mira, her elder girl, insists on trying for a scholarship to a university in Canada or the United States and has managed to wheedle money out of her daddy for the S.A.T.

With so many new sources of worry in Anita's life, the amicable twenty-year conjugality she has with her husband is the only thing she can count on. Some years from now, Anita's daughter Mira may question the assumptions and adjustments in her parents' marriage. She may find it strange that she never saw them hug or act playful, never heard them argue or shout. She may wonder how her so modern mother ungrudgingly accepted rushing back from work to do high-speed, single-handed battle in the kitchen, while her father, home earlier, fiddled with the TV or the short-wave radio or simply cushioned his head, propped his feet, and waited.

Yet there is no guarantee that Mira, ten years hence, will not find herself in similar circumstances and won over to her mother's rationale: she would have no trouble managing everything, if there were just thirty hours in the day.

PRIYA AND PADMA

"Going for shopping?"

Whenever we meet at the bus stop, that is Priya's conversation opener. Sometimes I am, though not in the pandemonium of the Colaba market, where Priya, faithful Bengali housewife, is going to haggle for a fresh fish for lunch. My destination is likely to be the Parsi emporium, where ten employees jump around bringing out brand names—Kleenex, Glad Bags, Philadelphia cream cheese. The owner is known to all upper-middle-class Bombay for his ability to procure fresh asparagus, authentic French camembert, and a reliable California chablis.

Such luxuries are not for Priya. Her weekly expenditure is budgeted down to the last paise, not through any meanness of her husband, but because his fixed monthly stipend is all there is. The list of strict necessities is long. There are the children's school tuition fees, school books, and uniforms; rent and electricity, and three compulsory savings plans: for health emergencies, for the once-a-year train trip to visit the elderly parents in Calcutta, and for eventual possession of a tiny apartment in a remote, and thus affordable, suburban tract.

Priya shops twice a day, six days a week. Each item—fish, mutton, vegetables, fruit, dry goods—comes from a different shop or stand, not necessarily all in walking distance of one another. There is also a problem of spoilage. Priya has an ancient General Electric refrigerator with a yellowed convex door on a faulty hinge; its mini-freezer compartment ices up cozy as an igloo in forty-eight hours. Priya's mornings are spent in cooking, shopping on foot or by bus, doing housework. After the noon meal and a short rest, she tries to get an hour's stitching done before it is time to supervise her children's homework, make them practice their Bengali, and return to the kitchen.

Enthroned in a corner of the bedroom is her new compact Japanese sewing machine, brought back by her husband's engineer brother who travels frequently to the Far East. Priya seems permanently in the midst of making a garment. There are fourteen young nieces and nephews to be remembered on birthdays and auspicious occasions. Priya finds solace and relaxation in sitting quietly at her machine, but she is often called away. Not by her boy or girl, who run out of doors the moment they've drunk their milk and dashed off their homework. But Priya is a good listener and a generous soul, and neighbors tend to drop by and stay for tea. In addition, she keeps an eye on Padma, whose many miscarriages have left her in delicate health. Sometimes Priya cooks enough to send a redolent fish curry upstairs. Padma's husband can never refuse a good *dahi machch.*

Only their child makes a fuss, ever since he got a taste of the United States. Padma's husband was sent to Rochester, New York, for a year's specialized training, and he brought his wife and child over on a tourist visa. Three months were enough for eight-year-old Anand to recognize the superiority of all things American, especially Chicken McNuggets. Now there are days when he categorically refuses to eat anything else. But neither the Parsi emporium nor the new fast food chain with its veg pizza and mutton cheeseburger has found the secret of the McNuggets crust. Padma makes a try, even though the mere look of raw meat turns her stomach. Who can say no to Anand, her jewel of a boy, her only liveborn child?

Priya privately considers Anand to be too pampered, even by the high standards of indulgence for a Bengali male. He is Gopal, the Divine Child, for whose health and safety his mother makes special devotions to the Lord Krishna. Only one child in the apartment complex is immune to Anand's pesty and vainglorious behavior, and that is Ritu, Priya's ten-year-old girl. Sassy and irrepressible, Ritu is the unchallenged leader of the grade-school pack that plays outside until nightfall in the open area behind the building. Priya's sensitivity about the carryings-on of her own daughter—where does that bold exuberance come from?—keeps her from making observations about Anand. For Ritu has simply exempted herself from all things feminine that constitute a girl's necessary apprenticeship. Her father tries to interest her in making a shoebox dollhouse decorated with scraps of fabric from Priya's remnant bag. Her auntie visits with her six-month-old and asks Ritu to help spoonfeed the little baby. "Ask brother to do it," calls Ritu, ducking out to rollerskate, or bike, or hang upside-down from the limb of a tree. Not a feminist in the bud, just a logical creature. Her brother is a quiet, dreamy boy; he might enjoy baby-tending.

Ritu will be twenty-one in the year 2001. Already, her approaching adolescence puts a frown on Priya's round, placid face. "If I don't give her some orientation, what will she do? How will she live?" Priya sees what is happening to the daughters and sons of her brother-in-law's wealthy colleagues. They are all smitten with America, anything American, indiscriminately. The blue jeans, the strange-looking shoes and hair-styles, all right. Times have changed. But they are getting so arrogant and opinionated, they talk back to their elders and demand all kinds of electronic gadgets. They sit around in fast food bars, and worse, they go in mixed groups to each other's homes to watch video films when there is no parent in the house. Priya and Padma's conversations very often come back to this: Of course, they want their children to have the best; but is the best a synonym for Made in USA?

Especially for an educated girl, there is the risk of making choices that cannot work. It is one thing to acquire legal rights and academic degrees, and it is quite another to find the social structures that correspond. A girl who is too educated is assumed headstrong; one too liberated from tradition, a threat to family harmony—in a word, unmarriageable. Priya cannot peer far enough ahead to see a time when a Hindu woman will find fulfillment separate from marriage and family life.

Whereas, within the economic and emotional haven of

marriage, many things are possible. A clever woman, as everyone knows, effectively holds the reins in the household. The home is her domain, and homemaking (as opposed to "outside" employment) is not devalued as in Western countries. "Whatever my husband has to say, I listen," said a housewife. "But ultimately he agrees to what I want. Any clever woman knows how to bring her husband around. By annoying a husband, a woman can never get anything out of him. With love and persuasion she is sure to win him over." [4]

Such a statement is remarkable for its echo of the *Kama Sutra* (IV,1) which outlines the duties of the housewife. As the primary household manager, she is to frame the budget, "put a gentle check on" the extravagance of her husband if he is a spendthrift; and if he is unable or unwilling to follow "the plain path of duty," she is to "bring him around by sweet yet effective words."

To defy or contradict a husband is undignified and "unfeminine"; but softening him up, wheedling concessions, shaming, or maneuvering him into a corner are recognized methods. The man must not lose face or have his authority overtly challenged. Tactics that many Western women consider demeaning are perceived as the self-respecting way, "our Indian women's way," as I was often told. Equality with the man is not an issue: women prefer to believe (or to behave as if they believed) their spouses to be, if not their earthly lords, in any case superior beings.

Priya points proudly to her eldest sister-in-law, Radha. Radha taught school before marriage and returned to her post when her youngest child was ten. Now she is principal of a leading girls' school. She battles the Bombay traffic at the wheel of her blue Maruti sedan, eats beef, chairs meetings, invests in the stock market. But every Tuesday she observes a total fast, taking only weak tea during the day. She has made this ritual sacrifice since the day she was married, to propitiate the gods or the fates who preserve the health and welfare of her husband and family. Whether Radha has faith in the effectiveness of her abstinence is not clear. She is matter-of-fact about it and is not otherwise "religious." She does not have household icons, perform daily prayer ceremonies, or observe the ritual events that Priya and Padma do. Propitiation may be instinctive in a land of so many obstructions and disasters. Yet, on meeting Radha and her family, I jumped to a more wicked conclusion. Radha is not only brighter, more dynamic, and independently wealthier than her husband—she is also two years his elder. She must be fasting, I cynically thought, to atone for her superiority.

But it is not that simple. Through the rite of fasting, which is by now so much a habit that she would not be able to tolerate a normal intake on a Tuesday, Radha situates her briskly paced contemporary life in the context of a nontemporal reality. From the vast impedimenta of Hindu tradition, she has selected an element that makes sense to her and bestows a larger dimension on her existence.

Preserving cultural continuities while rocketing ahead toward modernity is a preoccupation in India. Much seems to hinge upon women's not deviating from "tradition." Themes taken from the classic and sacred literature are simplified or debased to pound home this message. *Pati Parmeshwar* ("Husband, Lord Supreme"), a mass-market film produced in 1987, features a devout/devoted Hindu wife named Rekha. Her husband spends much of his time with his mistress, but Rekha does everything in her power to serve him and preserve their marriage. After the husband has been paralyzed in an accident, Rekha takes him to the other woman and looks after them both, in the hope that her goodness will make him see the light. It does. He repents, returns, and is accepted.

The only unpredictable thing about this film was that the Central Board of Film Certification banned it. A new guideline proscribes "visuals or words depicting women in ignoble servility to man or glorifying such servility as a praiseworthy quality." The film's producer challenged the ban before the Bombay High Court, claiming violation of freedom of expression guaranteed under Article 19 of the constitution. But more than that was at stake. "I believe that a marriage should be saved at all costs," he contended. "And the wife should make sacrifices. The Indian tradition is on trial."

The High Court judge revoked the ban. He found that Rekha "exemplified the inner strength of Indian womanhood." "If the film glorifies anybody," declared the actress who played Rekha, "it's the Indian woman. She achieves her goal through submission."[5]

Behind Radha's functional piety and Rekha's self-abasement, the same powerful machinery is at work. Aspiring to exemplify the ideal of womanhood is no illusion; making an effort, in any case, is just about mandatory. An all-powerful goddess lends her prestige and authority to the enterprise; and the heroines of the sacred literature provide inspirational demonstrations.

No Western culture places such potent, challenging, and ubiquitous role models before the eyes of its daughters. In Part Two, I shall recount the sagas of these female archetypes and illustrate their pertinence to the conduct of everyday life. It will then be possible to examine the abuses and to gauge the strength of the challenge being posed to traditional interpretations, through the vigorous resistance now showing forth among Indian women.

Part Two

In the mythologically instructed community there is a corpus of images and models that provide the pattern to which the individual may aspire, a range of metaphoric identity.

—Jerome S. Bruner,

MYTHS AND IDENTITY

✦7✦

FEMALE PROWESS: SHAKTI

On horseback and by chariot, nomadic tribes from steppe-lands to the north descended on the peaceful cities of the Indus Valley. Wave upon wave, during the millennium 2000 to 1000 B.C.E., the new settlers came. These light-skinned conquerors, the Aryans, brought a rich culture expressed in hundreds of religious hymns and chants called *Vedas* (a Sanskrit word meaning knowledge or wisdom). The Vedas were known only to the hereditary priests, who scrupulously memorized and passed them down orally from generation to generation. The myths and sacred rituals of these Aryan tribes, who worshiped sky gods, were markedly different from the religious practices of the conquered peoples of the Indus Valley. These latter had developed a flourishing agriculture-based civilization and venerated an earth goddess, a mother figure symbolized by the lotus, rather than a patriarchal deity.

Of the Vedic verses, the most significant collection is the 1,028 hymns of the *Rig-Veda,* probably composed between 1500 and 900 B.C.E. These texts elaborate a complex vision of the cosmos, the divinely ordained moral order, and its imperatives in human life. All that exists is but an illusory emanation of a Supreme Being existing from before the beginning of time—perhaps.

Then even nothingness was not, nor existence.
There was no air then, nor the heavens beyond it.
What covered it? Where was it? In whose keeping?
Was there then cosmic water, in depths unfathomed?

Then there were neither death nor immortality,
nor was there then the torch of night and day.

The One breathed windlessly and self-sustaining.
There was that One then, and there was no other. . . .

But, after all, who knows, and who can say
whence it all came, and how creation happened?
The gods themselves are later than creation,
so who knows truly whence it has arisen?

Whence all creation had its origin,
he, whether he fashioned it or whether he did not,
he, who surveys it all from highest heaven,
he knows—or maybe even he does not know. [1]

The unfathomable first principle, the Absolute Essence that preexists the gods, was called Brahman. Brahman is more remote than Allah, Jehovah, or the Father in the Christian trinity and impossible to represent anthropomorphically. More than Creator of the universe and Founder of a moral law, Brahman manifests itself *as* the universe yet preexists all universes, all time, all beginnings.

So vast and undefinable a being, whose nature cannot be conceived by the human imagination, is too austere a concept to inspire faith and devotion. But the infinite power of Brahman shapes its undifferentiated essence into a god, or any number of gods, and projects an aspect of itself as the universe in which the gods can operate. At this level myths are generated, of gods and demigods with their multifarious activities and relationships. These myths try to illuminate the beginnings of creation, the cyclical nature of time, and the illusory quality of human life, whose goal is liberation or deliverance from earth-bound experience.

Slowly, over the centuries of the Vedic period, a triadic deity evolved. As Aryan domination went on spreading eastward and southward, it not only influenced but was also altered by existing cults. The godhead that eventually emerged was the trinity of Brahma-Vishnu-Shiva. Three in one and one in three—it is a manifestation of the One Absolute. Brahma is the Creator (not the ultimate Brahm*an*, but merely the conduit, the actualization of the Absolute in the universe); Vishnu is Preserver and Conserver, and Shiva, god of Destruction in the sense of perpetual change, the death and dissolution necessary for continuous rebirth.

In current Hindu practice, Brahma plays a minor and largely historical role. Vast numbers of the faithful are devotees of Vishnu or Shiva. Their functions as Preserver and Destroyer are antagonistic and complementary; as such, they exemplify the marriage of opposites, a fundamental tenet of the Hindu worldview. There is nothing to preserve without the act of creation; what is created necessarily contains in it the seeds of destruction, the condition for the next cycle.

Vedic metaphysics is remarkable in its scope and its serene contemplation of billion-year time cycles. But it is not what has animated the religious fervor and inspired the exuberant art and architecture of Hindu India. For many centuries, the populace was ignorant of theological niceties. Vedic learning and access to the truth that makes men free was restricted to Sanskrit-speaking Brahmans, the scholars and priests. Brahmans are the top category of the four social divisions, the *varnas* (miscalled *castes*, which are in fact the many subdivisions of the four varnas). The Brahmans wrote down the sacred texts of the Vedas and the commentaries and interpretations that make up the *Upanishads*. What was retold in the vernacular and made accessible to the masses who comprised the lower varnas—soldiers, merchants, farmers, serfs—were the *Puranas* and the *Epics*. The Puranas ("ancient stories") are legends, religious tracts, and mythohistorical records variously collected and elaborated on for centuries and eventually compiled around the sixth century C.E. The Epics, whose first written versions date from the first few hundred years of our era, are the *Mahabharata*, attributed to the sage Vyasa, and the *Ramayana*, whose legendary author is Valmiki. These works are the immense storehouse of Hindu tradition.

But to backtrack a little. The Brahma-Vishnu-Shiva godhead, already complex, is made more so by the many manifestations and powers of each of its members. Vishnu in particular reappears throughout history. Among his ten reincarnations are Krishna and Buddha, deities worshiped in their own right. Furthermore, the Hindu god is not perceived as exclusively male, like Our Father in Heaven. Each Hindu divinity has a female component. Philosophically, this is the recognition that the Absolute embraces all divisions and dualities: male and female, antagonistic and complementary are reunited in the One. In popular worship, the female expression of godhead is personified as a separate goddess, endowed with specific virtues and powers. Thus Lakshmi, goddess of beauty, luck, and wealth, is the female aspect or consort of Vishnu; and Saraswati, protectress of learning and the arts, the female side of Brahma.

But in considering the Mahadevi—the great goddess consort of Shiva—we come to the most powerful expression of this polarity and synthesis. The great goddess incarnates the female aspect of the cosmic substance, which is called *shakti.* The noun shakti, from the Sanskrit root *śak,* signifies "to be able, to be possible." Shakti, in the instructive definition given by Heinrich Zimmer, is "power, ability, capacity, faculty, strength, energy, prowess; regal power; the power of composition, poetic power, genius; the power or signification of a word or term; the power inherent in cause to produce its necessary effect; an iron spear, lance, pike, dart; a sword." Zimmer adds, "Shakti is the female organ; shakti is the active power of a deity and is regarded, mythologically, as his goddess-consort and queen."[2]

In Hindu theology, the male aspect of divinity is all passive potential, dreamily absorbed in contemplating the enduring and absolute. Shakti, the female aspect, is the enabling energy, the dynamism. The relations between Shiva, god of destruction, and his Shakti—in her various manifestations as the goddesses Parvati, Durga, and Kali—provide a wealth of material for ethnological and psychoanalytic investigation well beyond the scope of this book.[3]

In India today, Mahadevi, or Devi, has far grander dimensions than simply goddess-consort of Shiva. Particularly in Bengal and in the South, she is worshiped independently of her cosmic husband. Major Hindu festivals, like Durga Puja, are consecrated to her. Her three manifestations make her a total exemplar of all aspects of womanhood. As Parvati, daughter of the Himalayas, she is the quintessence of feminine beauty and tender wifely devotion. Mother of Shiva's children, ever compliant and considerate, she is equally disposed for a millennium of uninterrupted lovemaking or several centuries of closely reasoned philosophical debate.

As Durga, she is a champion fighter, a warrior-goddess who intervenes, particularly to vanquish evil demons, which are, among other things, symbols of base human drives. She is thus the activated moral force of Shiva.

In her third and most ambiguous manifestation, she is Kali, goddess of destruction. Popularly depicted as dark-skinned, bedecked in a necklace of skulls and a girdle made of severed hands, she has a lolling red tongue, thirsty for hot blood. The many explicit portrayals of Kali performing a frenzied dance on the prostrate lifeless body of Shiva are a reminder that the Divine Absolute, when devoid of vitalizing energy, is inert, always potential, never procreative. Shiva the motionless and Kali the frenetically active symbolize the marriage of opposites in the ultimate unity of the Absolute.[4]

But the great goddess compels our interest at another level. Mother/lover/nurturer, moral guide and intercessor, and maniacal man-mutilator—are any male perceptions, desires, and fears of the female omitted in this all-purpose goddess? From idealized object of veneration to sexual predator smirched with blood, from protective and reliable mother to harmful and capricious mother, the great goddess fascinates and repels.

Where and when in the development of the mythology did this duality, female dynamism/male passivity, become a canon of Hinduism, henceforth to be elaborated in tales, temple sculpture, paintings, and today's omnipresent polychrome calendar art? And what contemporary conclusions can be drawn from the interpretations of this myth?

The first literary account of the great Devi is found in the *Markandeya Purana,* edited between the fourth and sixth century C.E. The notion of a powerful female goddess preexisted the Vedic conquest of India. No doubt the earth goddess of the indigenous agrarian peoples insinuated herself into the austere cosmogony of the Brahman elite, as the Aryans settled, mingled, and left off their nomadic ways. Among the minor female deities in the Rig-Veda is Vac, who is speech and whose precursor may be the pre-Vedic goddess Wa, meaning the Word. In the beginning was the Word: but, as reenvisioned by the Aryans, the female Vac must necessarily have been emitted by Brahman, thus setting the cosmos into motion. Zimmer posits the existence of a powerful goddess, "mother of the world," in India "long before the arrival of conquerers from the north."

> The occlusion of the Indus civilization together with its goddess queen must have resulted from the arrival of the strictly patriarchal warrior-herdsmen, and the installation of their patriarchal gods. The Mother was removed from her lotus and Brahma seated in her stead, she herself relegated . . . to the servile position of the brahmin wife. Nevertheless, in the hearts of the native population, her supremacy was maintained, and with the gradual merging, through the centuries, of the Vedic and pre-Vedic traditions, gradually she returned to her position of honor. She is visible everywhere in the monuments of early Buddhist art, and in the works of the classical period she stands triumphant on every side. Today she is the greatest power in the Orient. [5]

The legend that recounts the genesis of Shakti, "The Text of the Wondrous Essence of the Goddess," is related in the *Markandeya Purana.*

From time to time, potent demon kings would set upon the gods. The most formidable demon was Mahishasura, who took the shape of a colossal water buffalo bull. He and his legions managed to defeat the gods and force the whole pantheon out of heaven. The deposed gods prayed to the higher deities, Vishnu and Shiva. These great divinities swelled with wrath. From their rage emanated a great radiance. The other gods then proceeded to emit a hot and lustrous anger as well. A flaming cloud was formed, which condensed into the shape of an eighteen-armed goddess. Zimmer (190–191) then recounts:

> Upon beholding this most auspicious personification of the supreme energy of the universe, this miraculous amalgamation of all their powers, the gods rejoiced, and they paid her worship as their general hope. In her, . . . the perennial, primal Female, all the particularized and limited forces of their various personalities were powerfully integrated. Such an overwhelming totalization signified omnipotence. By a gesture of perfect surrender and fully willed self-abdication they had re-

> turned their energies to the primeval Shakti, the One Force, the fountain head, whence originally all had stemmed.

Each god then gave over one of his weapons or magic devices: Shiva his trident; Brahma his manuscript of the Vedas; Kala, god of time, his sword and shield. Thus did the host of the gods make the "cosmically significant gesture of willingly abdicating their various masculine attitudes—royal, valiant, and heroic—in order that the titan-demon may be destroyed. Into the hands of the Supreme Goddess they deliver their various weapons, utensils, ornaments and emblems. . . . Into the all-comprehending source out of which they themselves originally evolved, they now merge their disparate natures and disparate powers of action" (191).

Seated on a lion, the goddess rode forth to do battle with Mahishasura. The demon king took various forms, but each new transformation was annihilated by the goddess. At last, the demon resumed his bull shape. Strengthened by quaffing a bowl of the liquor of the life force, the goddess fell upon him and sent Shiva's trident through his neck. She then decapitated the beast and restored order to the universe.

This tale can be interpreted simply as demonstrating how the power inherent in Shiva expressed itself through his spouse. The goddess is nothing but the megaweapon contrived by the gods, their creature and emissary. She is also, in the end, in some way subjected to the demon bull. Iconic representations of Durga always include her killing the bull. Usually, both are smiling. Mahisha dies with a smile because his death releases him from doing evil; Durga the Redeemer has saved the evildoer from himself. But she can never be free of him. For, once the bull was in her power, Durga had relented enough—in her womanly way?—to grant him a boon. His wish was that she not destroy his body. Thus, sculptures and paintings of Durga always include the bull's body. In this way, the demon shares in the worship offered to the goddess. I will offer some further comment on this, after describing the next tale—one of the most celebrated and often-depicted episodes in the legend of the Goddess Durga, Shiva's Shakti—from the *Markandeya Purana*.

Yet another band of demons had succeeded in snatching

the sacrificial offerings that had been set out for the gods. Deprived of their function, the gods were obliged to vacate heaven. Off they went to a sacred mountain to invoke the goddess in hymns of praise and entreaty. The great goddess Parvati appeared to them. From the sheath of her body, the *kosha,* sprang a very beautiful goddess, Kaushiki. All the demons immediately coveted her. She would marry the one who could defeat her in battle, Kaushiki declared.

The demon chiefs sent their warriors, whom Kaushiki decimated. But the last demon remaining, Raktabija, had her momentarily stymied. Every drop of his blood that fell to earth gave rise to another, stronger Raktabija. From the frown of her forehead, Kaushiki projected another self, Kali. To Kali she suggested that the only solution was to catch the drops of blood before they could reach the ground. Kali, mouth agape and tongue protruding, lapped each drop, as the flashing sword of Kaushiki finished off the demons.

In the Mahishasura myth, the goddess is seen to be the creature of the male gods, conjured up for a specific need. Although the gods are powerless without her, they do not install her in their midst, and when they are in trouble, they must look for her again. In the Raktabija episode, the goddess seems to go it alone, launching her own permutations and mowing down demons left and right.

Here, the focus is of course on the popular perceptions of these myths, not the erudite interpretations, that would doubtless uncover layers of meaning vital to understanding Hindu philosophy. No icon in Indian art or event in the literature is simple or unidimensional—and that is its richness and fascination. But here I aim to see how these cherished tales instruct the minds of ordinary people, not scholars. As a frame of reference, one can recall the Hindu view of the creative conflict of opposites at play within a unified divine essence, beyond our conceiving, yet immanent in our souls. On a less rarefied level, ancient tales can be read through contemporary lenses to gain fresh perspectives about their origins and pertinence.

A suggestive reading of the two myths has been proposed by an Indian anthropologist, Veena Das. As already noted, when the goddess slew the bull demon, her act of grace was to conserve his body. In this way, Das points out, the demonic forces, qualities of darkness known as *tamas,* remain forever associated with the goddess Durga. In the tale of Raktabija, the goddess is not only in touch with the demonic, but she imbibes it. According to the Puranic text, after drinking the blood, the goddess "appeared to bear a resemblance to a demoness." Das suggests that the threat posed to the moral order of the world by demonic forces is dispelled by the female principle's absorbing these forces into herself. As the goddess becomes more autonomous and less a creature of the gods, the distance also grows between the gods and the demons. The gods become stainless, uninvolved, cosmically disinterested, while the goddess presents an enigma. By nature she who embodies purity *(sattvas)* is also tainted with *tamas,* the negative and sordid.[6]

Herein is exemplified the treacherous nature of the female. On the one hand she is devoted, self-disciplined (chaste), and ready to sacrifice (for men); on the other, she is sexual, anarchic, destructive, and bloody. The most striking popular image of this is Kali, going amok, roused by the hot blood of the demon and about to raise havoc with the universe. Shiva throws himself at her feet in a last-ditch effort to stop her. Not only will he impede her with his body, but he also hopes that the consciousness of trampling on the chest of her lord will sober Kali's frenzy and call forth her loving aspect.

The more scholarly interpretation of this scene was cited above. But the fact is that Kali's orgiastic dance on the body of Shiva is a favorite subject of devotional art. In the popular imagery, the goddess Parvati/Durga/Kali is the female paradigm. Part of her inherent contradiction lies in her being the shakti of Shiva. Shiva, simultaneously creator and destroyer, is a more ambiguous god than Vishnu, the preserver. Equally less ambiguous are the goddesses who constitute Vishnu's shakti, chiefly the faithful Lakshmi. Yet, while many millions of Hindus pay homage to Shiva or Vishnu, only one goddess has as vast and fervent a following—Durga/Kali. As patron saint of Calcutta, that most hallucinatory of Indian cities, her intervention is most sought, her fury most feared. Her caprices are an endless source of admiration and alarm.

A very powerful lady is Durga/Kali. Men, helpless before

her, cringe in their inadequacy, bow to her will, and vie to do her bidding. This aspect of female prowess can operate, in India, on secular and political planes. The ascendancy of the late Indira Gandhi in some ways exemplifies the working out of this identification. Nothing in the Hindu culture prevents a forceful woman—intelligent, ambitious, ideally well-connected, and with a "manifest destiny"—from mounting to the top, where she is surrounded by praise and entreaty. Male politicians promptly surrender to her. There is neither embarrassment nor a sense of inappropriateness in this displacement of the Hindu habit of devotion.

At the same time, ordinary women, whatever their portion of goddesslike power, must be subordinated and constrained. One recalls that the authors of all the venerated texts were elite Brahman males, who were just as fastidious about the lower orders of society as they were leery of women. Thus, they faced a dilemma. The female was the mother, wife, and nurturer, perpetuator of the clan, the race. How was her vital force to be channeled along strictly generative, ritually sanctioned lines?

In the next chapters, we see how Sita, the exemplary wife in the *Ramayana,* and Draupadi, the heroine of the *Mahabharata,* proceed to recognize or deny, manifest or suppress their prodigious womanly powers. The interactions of these archetypal Hindu women with husbands and in-laws, with enemies and would-be ravishers, and with the very gods themselves, are the stuff of Hindu folklore, and they supply a large part of everyone's cultural diet. Children read of them in comic books, hear the tales from elders, enact episodes in school pageants, view them on television; they know them more intimately than we know Mother Goose. Together with the Hindu goddesses, the Epic women broadcast a message that is both tonic and intimidating. It credits a girl/woman with a sense of her own vivid potential and worth. And it enjoins her—as a cosmic responsibility—to channel this force within fixed, inviolable bounds.

8

FEMALE PROPRIETY: STREEDHARMA

Who is Sita? She is the heroine of the *Ramayana*, an action-packed tale in which the representatives of Good (the ordained way, dharma) are pitted against all manner of foe, from scheming relatives and corrupt advisers to hostile demigods and man-eating demons. Its hero is Prince Rama, who, though mortal, is unbeknownst to himself an incarnation of the god Vishnu. He radiates courage and virtue, and his faithful brother Lakshman is a model of selfless devotion. Their ally is the monkey king, Hanuman, in recognition of whose valiant deeds, monkeys are considered sacred animals in India.

The tale, with its grandeur and carnage, its mix of mortals and divines, contains the seeds of much universal folklore. Among the familiar elements are ominous natural portents, forests full of monsters, banishment and ascetic wanderings as tests of courage and merit. But throughout there is a distinctly Indian hallmark—the aura of piety. The *Ramayana* is not just a good yarn or even an allegorical tale: intended to edify, it is full of digressions into theology, morals, and statecraft. One scholar has suggested that both the *Ramayana* and the *Mahabharata* originated as martial legends, which were "worked over by a succession of priestly editors." [1]

Abridged editions of the saga published in India for home consumption take up the didactic mission. In his widely read English version, the late statesman-scholar C. Rajagopalachari does not hesitate to heap his own well-intentioned asides onto the message in the text. Thus, just after a particularly dramatic episode, the translator steps in to comment: "To millions of men, women and children in India, the *Ramayana* is not a mere tale. It has more truth and meaning than the events in one's own life. Just as plants grow under the influence of sunlight, the people of India grow in mental strength and culture by absorbing the glowing inspiration of the *Ramayana*."[2]

A contemporary Indian psychiatrist makes the same observation from a different viewpoint. "It is through the recitation, reading, listening to, or attending a dramatic performance of this revered text (above all others) that a Hindu reasserts his or her cultural identity as a Hindu and obtains religious merit. The popular epic contains ideal models of familial bonds and social relations to which even a modernized Hindu pays lip service, however much he may privately question or reject them as irrelevant to the tasks of modern life."[3] Small wonder that the *Ramayana*, with wicked, mustachioed villains and modest, sumptuous maidens, is a best-seller in the *Amar Chitra Katha* ("Immortal Comics") series, and the Sunday morning television serial version is followed with fanatic devotion.

Here are the elements of the story. The childless king Janaka, while plowing his field, had found a baby girl in a furrow. He adopted her and named her Sita.[4] She grows up to become a beautiful princess. Many princes compete for her hand, but Rama is the only one who is able to bend, and snap in two, the golden bow that no other suitor can even lift off the ground. Sita marries Rama. The words intoned by Sita's father at the wedding ceremony are repeated at Hindu marriage rites even to this day.[5]

Rama, as the eldest son of King Dasaratha, is the rightful heir to his father's throne. But because of a pledge made by the aged king to the jealous mother of another of the sons, Rama must be banished to the forest for fourteen years. He urges Sita to remain comfortably in the palace and await his return. But she refuses, saying: "For a woman, it is not her father, her son, nor her mother, friends, nor her own self, but the husband who in this world and the next is ever her sole means of salvation. If thou dost enter the impenetrable forest today, . . . I shall precede thee on foot, treading down the spiky kusha grass. In truth, whether it be in palaces, in chariots or in heaven, wherever the shadow of the feet of her consort falls, it must be followed."[6]

Accompanied by Rama's younger brother Lakshman, they set off for the forest. For many years they live as nomads, dressed in bark, eating fruits and roots, and helping righteous creatures whom they meet to fend off monstrous demons. Eventually, the two brothers come upon the sister of Ravanna, demon-king of Lanka. [7] The ten-headed Ravanna is a satanic character with supernatural powers that derive from his former status as a god. By neglecting the sacrifices and flouting the dharma, he has become an antigod. His sister tries to seduce Rama and Lakshman, but they spurn her advances. Furious, she demands that her brother avenge her.

Ravanna, who has for some time been coveting Sita, now devises a plan to kidnap her. He sends a demon in the shape of a golden deer to roam near the hut of the heroes. Sita, entranced, prevails on Rama to chase the beautiful animal. The hunt leads Rama far from the hut. At last, he shoots an arrow into the neck of the deer. At its dying moment, the creature screams in perfect imitation of Rama's voice, "Sita! Lakshman! Help!"

Sita is overwhelmed with fear and urges Lakshman to rush to Rama's aid. But Lakshman has promised his elder brother never to leave Sita's side. He tries to persuade her that the voice is very likely a ruse and that no real harm has befallen Rama. Sita becomes frantic. She accuses Lakshman of the worst: he is a false friend, a false brother, an imposter. Reluctantly Lakshman chides her for behaving like an ordinary woman, quick to think evil of others. Sita's riposte is that she will kill herself before his eyes unless he goes to rescue Rama. Compelled to disobey his brother in order to honor the will of his sister-in-law, he leaves, pausing only to draw around the hut a white circle that Sita, for her own safety, is forbidden to cross.

Immediately there appears a holy beggar, who is none other than Ravanna in one of his transformations. Bearing all the outward signs of a true yogi, he has Vedic hymns on his lips but lust in his heart. Sita dutifully offers water and food to the holy man. In so doing, she crosses the fatidic line. Ravanna, in his real guise, sweeps her up by the hair, lifts her into his airborne chariot, and whisks her off to Lanka.

The rest of the tale recounts the efforts of the two heroes to locate and rescue Sita, with the help of the great monkey army of Hanuman and timely assistance from the gods. Sita, meanwhile, remains prisoner in Ravanna's luxurious palace. At first, he tries to woo her, desiring her love, not just her body. Perhaps there is an inkling of redemption here: the love of a pure woman might improve his position in the eternal cycle of rebirths. More immediate is his awareness of the curse to which he is subject. He is forbidden to possess a woman by force, on pain of irrevocable death. Ravanna humbles himself before Sita and offers to rid himself of all other wives, give her all his wealth, and make himself her slave.

Her reply is exemplary. "You ask me to accept you. How foolish! Can the crow approach the swan? Can a heinous sinner be allowed near the sacrificial fire? I do not value life or body. Do you imagine I would wish to live despised by the world? Do not dream that out of fear or to save my life I shall yield to you." [8]

Ravanna grows angry. He gives Sita twelve months in which to change her mind—or be eaten by him for breakfast—and sets her up in a walled garden. Here, for several months, grotesque demon guardians subject her to psychological punishment, alternating threats and temptations, inventing grisly scenarios to break her will. The she-demons particularly deride and provoke her; perhaps they are caricatures of the envious sisters-in-law of the youngest, loveliest bride.

Sita remains adamant, though not without moments of despair and fleeting notions of suicide. But her faith in Rama sustains her, and before the twelve months are out the forces of good descend on Lanka. There is general mayhem, the city is reduced to ashes, and tens of thousands are killed. At last, Ravanna, who has effortlessly survived a tenfold beheading, falls to Rama, who is reinforced by a magic weapon sent special delivery from the gods. Rama and Lakshman then return to their camp and ask that Sita be brought to them.

But it is a tense and solemn reunion. "Aryaputra," whispers Sita ("Beloved and noble one"—the intimate and respectful form of address of a highborn wife to her husband). But Rama's look is cold. "By killing Ravanna," he says, "I have wiped away the insult to our family and to myself, but you are stained by dwelling with one other than myself. What man of high degree receives back a wife who has lived long in another's house? Ravanna has held you on his lap and gazed on you with lustful eyes. I have avenged his evil deed, but I am unattached to you; O gentle one, I am forced by a sense of honor to renounce you."[9]

Depending on the version one reads, Sita grows either tearful or angry, either tries to convince Rama of her rectitude or demands its immediate demonstration. She calls for a huge fire to be kindled and throws herself onto the blaze. Agni, god of fire, forbids his flames to touch her. Sita is purity itself: there is nothing to burn.

With joy in his heart, Rama takes Sita back. Again, versions differ. Some translators accept Rama's declaration: "Because this beautiful woman remained in Ravanna's clutches it was necessary for her innocence to be made clear in front of all people. If I had taken her back without any hesitation, people could have said that I did so out of desire and passion, and I would thus have been a bad example."[10] Rama is credited with conviction in his inner heart that Sita is chaste but obligation, as king and guardian of the dharma, to prove to the people both Sita's purity and his own austere devotion to principle.

Other interpreters suspect Rama of having real misgivings, of displaying sexual jealousy and a selfish interest in keeping his own dharma-record clean. Sita is then credited with the sheer disinterested courage of a martyr entering the flames.

This latter reading finds support in an episode appended to the story at a later date. It recounts how, after some time, Rama again—through personal doubts or to stanch real or imagined rumors—banishes the now pregnant Sita to a distant forest. There again she lives simply and meekly and raises her twin sons. Only after seeing the children does Rama wish to have Sita repeat the ordeal by fire, to lay all doubts incontrovertibly to rest. But here Sita draws the line: one trial by fire is enough. She calls upon her mother, earth, to swallow her up and disappears into the furrow from whence she came.

Different explanations are offered in discussions of Rama's

second, unjustifiable demand. Some suggest that once Rama had slain Ravanna, his purpose as a god-incarnation was fulfilled, and losing his divine aspect, he became an ordinary, flawed mortal. Others, like Rajagopalachari, note, as if with a sigh, that this episode can only "mirror the voiceless and endless suffering of our womenfolk" (311).

Throughout the story, Rama and Lakshman display unwavering courage and suffer constant anguish. But the two men frequently benefit from instructions or tactical aid from gods, who keep them clearheaded about the demands of their dharma, their destiny as warrior princes. Sita, captive in the walled garden, harassed by harpies, has only her *stree-dharma* as guide—her inner, implicit knowledge of how to comport herself as a worthy Hindu wife. This, her great and eternal merit, is held up for emulation by women today. Sita's qualities are praised in devotional songs; her name is synonymous with purity, patience, and self-sacrifice.

In a study made in 1960 in the state of Uttar Pradesh, 500 young men and 360 young women between the ages of nine and twenty-two were asked to select their ideals from a list of twenty-four names of gods, goddesses, heroes, and heroines. An overwhelming majority of respondents, irrespective of age or sex, selected Sita as the ideal woman. [11] "Her unique standing in the minds of most Hindus, regardless of region, caste, social class, age, sex, education or modernization, testifies to the power and pervasiveness of the traditional idea of womanhood." [12]

Of course, the *Ramayana* is the production of a male elite, the perpetuating guardians of a patriarchal society. In it women's behavior conforms to the brahmanic projection of the way things should be. But "very early in childhood, girls learn to accurately perceive and conform to the patriarchal images of femininity entertained by the men around them in the household." [13] This is more than the desire to be "daddy's good girl," which plays a role in the behavior of young girls everywhere. The Sita ideal is part of a Hindu woman's psychic inheritance, and she inculcates it, both overtly and unwittingly, in her daughters. Not only does a girl learn to bear cheerfully and without complaint all kinds of discomfort, injustice, and misfortune, but she also deduces that one does not defy, berate, or expect too much of men. As Sudhir Kakar notes (66), the Sita legend provides a glimpse of the Hindu imagery of manliness. Rama, with all his godlike heroic traits, is emotionally fragile, mistrustful, and jealous, very much a conformist to general opinion.

What one can extrapolate from the Epics shows that real relations between everyday men and women fell far short of the brahmanic ideal. Passages in the *Mahabharata* depict women as sexually insatiable, full of lust.

> The fire has never too many logs,
> the ocean never too many rivers,
> death never too many living souls,
> and fair-eyed woman never too many men. [14]

Husbands are enjoined to keep a lookout, or else their wives will consort with any passing stranger. Women are regarded as fickle, capricious, resentful, and quarrelsome.

This is one side of the story. Woman is also vaunted as man's best friend, safest refuge, source of courage, comfort, and salvation. One verse cautions,

> Even a man in the grip of rage
> will not be harsh to a woman,
> remembering that on her depend
> the joys of love, happiness, and virtue. [15]

The *Laws of Manu,* the most famous Sanskrit treatise on human conduct, clearly exhibits the polarized male perception of the female. Written by one historical individual in the early centuries of our era, this treatise is the first of the *Dharma Shastras,* verse-form instructions in the sacred law. In minute detail it lays down the rules of conduct, the privileges and obligations of each division of society, and penalties and punishments for wrong or inappropriate behavior. The law applies a strict brahmanic standard, which legitimizes inequality and protects the interests of the ruling class. Regarding women, nothing is left uncodified. Marriage is indissoluble, divorce impossible, and widow remarriage never permitted to "respectable women." As for adultery—if the man involved is of base caste, the woman should be torn apart by dogs.

There is historical evidence that the lower classes, peasants and artisans, paid less attention to these prohibitions than did "respectable" society. Love marriages, divorce, and widow remarriage discreetly took place among them. Manual and agricultural work made them less fastidious and more pragmatic, perhaps, than the Brahman elite. They might have taken with a grain of salt Manu's dire warning that if a man approaches a woman "covered with menstrual excretions," then his wisdom, energy, strength, might, and vitality would "utterly perish." [16]

Manu's laws were imposed as *the* Hindu law code by the eighteenth-century colonial governor Warren Hastings, in consultation with Brahman priests. This measure is seen today as violating the more flexible, local customs, which gave wider latitude and imposed fewer constraints on women, especially non-Brahmans. But Manu has given posterity a celebrated portrait of the compleat Hindu woman (i.e., wife, for at the time of his writing, the two were synonymous). Here the Sita ideal is grafted—because most wives are not princesses—onto that of the perfect homemaker.

> She should do nothing independently
> even in her own house.
> In childhood subject to her father,
> in youth to her husband,
> and when her husband is dead to her sons,
> she should never enjoy independence. . . .
>
> She should always be cheerful,
> and skilful in her domestic duties,
> with her household vessels well cleansed,
> and her hand tight on the purse-strings. . . .
>
> In season and out of season
> her lord, who wed her with sacred rites,
> ever gives happiness to his wife,
> both here and in the other world.
>
> Though he be uncouth and prone to pleasure,
> though he have no good points at all,

the virtuous wife should ever
worship her lord as a god.—trans. Basham (180–181)

That these stanzas are still held to apply can be seen in a film like *Pati Parmeshwar* and in the charges and countercharges in divorce and wife-abuse cases. Accused husbands justify even criminal behavior in terms that show a self-serving adhesion to Manu's dicta. Yet neither the Epics nor Manu conceived of wifely devotion as a one-way street. The husband, like the king, or like the higher varnas in the feudal relations of the time, has the firm responsibility to be benevolent and paternal with the women of his household. As Manu writes: "Where women are honored, there gods are pleased; but where they are not honored, no sacred rite yields rewards. . . . Where the female relations live in grief, the family soon wholly perishes; but that family where they are not unhappy ever prospers." [17]

The idyllic reciprocity between enlightened master and faithful vassal is rarely achieved in the domestic sphere. Women described as capricious, vengeful, and sly might simply be the suppressed and disenfranchised, finding covert ways to protest. Confined to the home compound, the various sisters-in-law and co-wives were bound to quarrel, cheat, and connive. Despotic powers often were, and still are, exercised by a mother-in-law or eldest brother's wife, risen at last to a queenly position over the other wives, not-yet-married children, and widowed relatives under the joint-family roof.

Highly charged and ambivalent terms apply to woman as perceived as a sexual being. Everything changes when woman transmutes into mother, for mother, according to the Hindu ideal and Manu's text, is something distinctly different. "A spiritual teacher exceeds a worldly teacher ten times, a father exceeds a spiritual teacher one hundred times, but a mother exceeds a thousand times a father's claim to honor on the part of a child as its educator." [18]

The ability to give birth and sustain life, to conceive sons and assure the continuity of the lineage, is woman's supreme virtue. Here attitudes that began, just as in other cultures, in the tribal need to multiply in the face of immense odds, prevail today in a land whose greatest single obstacle to a decent life is its birthrate. The Indian reverence for motherhood and for mother figures, the respectful form of addressing older women as "Mother," and the shame attached to childlessness are characteristic. More than one birth control campaign has foundered on these shoals.

By becoming a mother, the Hindu woman does much more than procreate. She compensates for the misfortune of being born female. She redeems her stock, improves her standing at home and in society, confirms her cultural status, and gains some degree of freedom, especially if she has produced sons. By all rights, Sita too should have enjoyed these rewards and lived happily ever after as a mother and queen. The respect and devotion of her sons would have compensated for the lapses of her husband—as can happen in an Indian family. By producing two male heirs at once, Sita seems to have given even further proof of her perfect fidelity to Rama and her aptness to accede to the status of mother.

But this was to no avail, if one is to heed the addendum *(Uttarakanda)* of the *Ramayana,* where Rama once again calls her to account. Now, however, Sita refuses to replay the ordeal-by-fire scenario and sets her own terms for demonstrating her virtue. "If in thought, I have never dwelt on any but Rama, may the Goddess [Earth] receive me!" [19] These are fatal words, for Sita knows how truly single-minded she has been. The phrasing reverses the usual terms of a challenge, wherein one asks to be struck down or swallowed up if one has *not* fulfilled a bargain or duty. It is tempting to read this as a sign that even Sita comes at last to a point of wanting to be done with being Sita, and she devises an elegant, ultimate act of rebellion, worthy of herself.

◆9◆

THE EPIC WIFE

The *Mahabharata* is the epic of epics, the longest poetic composition in world literature, eight times the length of *Illiad* and the *Odyssey* combined. It recounts the lifelong rivalry between two clans of warrior princes. Interspersed in the narrative of intrigues and battles is much independent material: legends, instruction manuals for kings, and philosophic discourses, the best known of which is the *Bhagavad Gita*. The heroine of the tale, Draupadi, is a personage unique in Hindu literature.

The five Pandava brothers, who have been banished from their rightful kingdom by their rival cousins the Kauravas, are living in exile and disguised as Brahman ascetics. They spend their days begging for alms, which they take home each evening to their mother, to be divided equitably among them.

A ceremonial contest for the hand of the king's daughter, Draupadi, is about to take place. The successful candidate must string a heavy bow and shoot five arrows into a revolving target, seen only in reflection. The Kauravas enter the competition, but none of them is able to perform the deed. Arjuna, the gifted archer of the Pandavas, then steps up, strings the bow, and hits the target at each shot. He wins the fair lady.

Arjuna and his brothers bear Draupadi home to their mother. Bhima, the most jocular of the five, calls from outside the door, "Oh, Mother, wait till you see what alms we got today!" Without looking up from her cooking, Kunti, the mother, says, "Share it out and enjoy it among yourselves as usual."

And the mother's word becomes law. Neither her protestations—once she realizes what is at stake—nor the horrified refusal of Draupadi's father can dissuade Arjuna from his contention that Mother must be obeyed. The eldest brother, Yudhisthira, concurs. He has already observed how his younger brothers are eying the young beauty and covertly looking at one another, how the god of desire has "invaded their hearts and crushed all their senses." Without hesitation, he decrees, "The auspicious Draupadi shall be the common wife of us all."[1]

Yudhisthira, who is known for his moral rectitude, has recalled that a seer once predicted something along these lines. Polyandrous marriage is not only a way to avoid dispute but also seemingly a matter of predestination. Draupadi's father, the king, may well protest that, though one man can take many wives, "one woman taking several husbands has never been approved anywhere, either in practice or in the scriptures." Yudhisthira is unmoved: "The right way is subtle and complicated. I know I am not deviating from it. . . . Have no misgivings."[2]

At this point, the sage Vyasa, the supposed author of the epic, who also wanders through it making comments from time to time, arrives on the scene. In private, he recounts to the king a curious tale.[3] Draupadi, he explains, was, in her former incarnation, Nalayani, a chaste and pious woman. She was married to a sage who was not only filthy and repulsive to look at but also despotic, choleric, and altogether insupportable. But support him she did, obeying his commands, submitting to his moods, eating the scraps he threw her—and all this, "without hesitation or mental protest, totally effacing her own ego."

After many years, the day came for the husband to reveal his true self: handsome, virile, and young. "Oh perfect wife, you have passed through the severest trial and come through unscathed. I assumed this vicious and disgusting appearance to test you, and you are the most forebearing partner a man could hope for." And he declared he would grant her any boon she wished.

Unfazed, Nalayani requested that henceforth he love her as five men, in five different forms, yet always coming back to and merging into one. And so he did. The two of them set off to live a life of perpetual pleasure, travel, and romance.

L'amour toujours—until one day he decided he had had enough: it was time for him to retire into solitary introspection. Nalayani was furious, "insatiate." But her husband, as R. K. Narayan puts it, "warded her off as a drag on his spiritual progress."

Nalayani then concentrated all the force of her passion into rigorous meditation. At length, the god appeared to her and asked what she desired. "My husband," she said. "My husband, husband, husband, husband."

"You will be reborn on earth and marry five husbands."

"(!!!!)," as an Immortal Comics version would have Nalayani reply.

But the gods don't joke. Draupadi, the reincarnation, cheerfully takes up her role in the cosmic scenario.

Some scholars suggest that Draupadi's marriage harks back to a matriarchal culture based on polyandry that might have flourished long before. But no one really knows how this astonishing circumstance finds itself at the core of the *Mahabharata*. Equally striking is Draupadi's character as it develops. She is probably the most complex and controversial female in ancient Hindu literature. From her previous incarnation, she retains not only the verve and the appetite but also the capacity for unstinting service.

In Draupadi's life with the Pandavas, the erotic aspect is subordinate to the companionate and the housewifely. She is shared out according to a strict schedule, one full year for each husband, on a basis of exclusive rights. During this time, the others must practice a refined form of detachment and discipline, eradicating all intimate thoughts or images of her from their minds.

Although Draupadi complies with this program, there are indications that she is not entirely impartial. Arjuna, the handsome archer who won her, is the most attractive to her sexually. For the colossal Bhima, who strikes blows rather than split hairs and frequently comes to her rescue, she feels the affectionate trust of a sister. Yudhisthira, the most subtle and intellectual, stimulates her intelligence and sharpens her mettle; he provokes the events that reveal Draupadi's range of virtues.

Yudhisthira has a single weakness, an Achilles' heel. As a

compulsive gambler, he accepts his deceitful cousins' challenge to a game of dice. The Kauravas have fixed the match, and one by one, Yudhisthira stakes and loses all his possessions, his kingdom, the clothes off his back; at last, he stakes his wife. When this ultimate throw of the dice is lost, Draupadi is sent for. But she refuses to leave the women's quarters, arguing that, if Yudhisthira had already staked and lost kingdom and title, then she, Draupadi, was no longer his to stake. Several times summoned, Draupadi raises a number of protests and moral questions, but to no avail. She then admits to the rough messenger who has come for her that she is in her monthly period and not appropriately clothed to appear before an assembly of men.

But her objections are futile: princess or not, she is dragged by the hair into the arena. Dressed in the simple garment one might wear at home when indisposed, she is jostled and insulted by the Kaurava crowd. Still, she puts up a good fight, challenging the nature of the match, denouncing the cowardice of her husbands, reviling the assembled cousins. Only when the extremes of cruelty are reached—she is accused of being a public woman, a whore, and commanded to disrobe—does she break down. Her husbands appear impotent to help her; she can only call upon other-worldly intercession. She cries out to Krishna, an incarnation of the god Vishnu, and surrenders her will into his hands.

And Krishna contrives for her sari to become endless. Each length that is unwound reveals another, and as the pile of cloth mounts higher and higher and the victim remains fully clothed, the audience is taken aback. The old king, father of the Kauravas, repents of all that has taken place and praises Draupadi for her courage and virtue. He will grant her any favor she asks.

"Free Yudhisthira from slavery," is her immediate reply.

"Granted. You may ask another."

"Let all his brothers be freed."

"Granted." The remorseful king tells her she may have one more boon.

Draupadi, in her great self-abnegation—or in her great self-respect—coolly turns him down. "I don't want anything more," she says.

The brothers, given back their possessions, are let go. It is a temporary respite. Another crooked match soon follows, and the Pandava family, again stripped of their wealth, go into twelve years' exile in the forest.

During their exile, they have ample leisure for reflection and discourse. Draupadi not only joins in but also initiates philosophical discussions with Yudhisthira. In particular, she considers the relative merits of mercy and revenge, a matter of urgent moment for Yudhisthira. She argues like a lawyer, citing learned sources and historical precedents; she challenges her husband's judgment, plays on his emotions.[4] Sometimes her incentive brings the other brothers, ever cautious and respectful, into the argument.

At the same time, Draupadi is proud to describe herself as *streedharmini,* a loyal and faithful wife, and to recount fully what that entails. At one point, another noble lady takes Draupadi aside to ask, "By what behavior is it that thou art able to rule the sons of Pandu? . . . How is it that they are so obedient to thee and never angry with thee? Without doubt they . . . are ever submissive to thee and watchful to do thy bidding!"[5]

Here, with some minor deletions, is Draupadi's reply.

> Keeping aside vanity, and controlling desire and wrath, I always serve with devotion the sons of Pandu with their wives. Restraining jealousy, with deep devotion of heart, without a sense of degradation at the services I perform, I wait upon my husbands. Ever fearing to utter what is evil or false, or to look or walk with impropriety, or cast glances indicating the feelings of the heart, do I serve. . . . Celestial or man, young or decked with ornaments, wealthy or comely of person, none else my heart liketh. I never bathe or eat or sleep til he that is my husband hath bathed or eaten or slept. . . . I always keep the house and all household articles and the food that is to be taken well-ordered and clean. Carefully do I keep the rice, and serve the food at the proper time.

She goes on to report that she never indulges in fretful speech, never lingers at the gates of the compound or in the gardens. "When my husband leaves home for the sake of any relative, then renouncing flowers and fragrant paste of every kind, I begin to undergo penances. Whatever my husband enjoyeth not, I ever renounce. . . . Those duties that my mother-in-law has told me in respect of relatives, of almsgiving, of offering worship to the gods . . . I always discharge day and night, without idleness of any kind." In sum: "My husbands have become obedient to me in consequence of my diligence, my alacrity, and the humility with which I serve superiors."

At first glance, it looks like the impossible ideal being trotted out again. Yet, what struggle for self-mastery, what counterimpulses are suggested. "Keeping aside vanity," "controlling desire and wrath," "restraining jealousy," "without a sense of degradation." A sizable amount of emotion has been repressed, or transformed, or transcended. Draupadi may not permit herself to cast loaded glances or respond to other men who pass her way, but her eyes do not fail to see them. Performing so many duties and services and warding off aggressive feelings must indeed keep her busy, and thus "without idleness," day and night. She never pauses, even momentarily, to reflect on her situation, a situation of both necessity and choice. Indeed, her peak performance gives Draupadi a sense of pride and self-worth; at the same time it assures her the esteem of her husbands.

In general, Draupadi strikes a more modern chord than does Sita. Less malleable and less accommodated to her sufferings than Sita is, Draupadi is also a more powerful personality: quick-witted and confident. In the text, together with the many references to her physical beauty, she is frequently called "spirited." Draupadi's character may well reflect what the ancient spinners of the tale observed of their own mothers, sisters, and wives: the elite women of the time. In the narrative, Draupadi appears in everyday interactions with family and friends. By contrast, in the *Ramayana,* Sita is often seen in the process of being subordinated and intimidated by a male. In Draupadi's words and actions one senses an ambivalence, a nay (nipped in the bud, of course) that is perhaps tacitly recognized by the tellers of the tale. We do not find this in Sita, the innocent and pious, who lowers her eyes and does not raise her voice. Why then is Sita and not Draupadi—who has so many character traits in common with today's elite women—perceived as the ideal of Hindu womanhood?

One evident contrast between the two paragons is in their sexuality. The modest Sita is a one-man woman; the sensuous Draupadi lives out an enviable sexual fantasy—variety without insecurity, gratification without guilt. Draupadi may be closer to modern sensibilities, but Sita is safer stuff to work with.

Among the mass-produced polychrome prints sold everywhere in India, those that depict morally elevating scenes from the two epics—the marriage of Rama and Sita, Ravanna's abduction of Sita, and Sita in the flaming pyre—are among the most popular. The only image of Draupadi is the undressing scene, where Krishna above is rewarding her faith and protecting her virtue. In the *Mahabharata* itself, the women eventually fade offstage as the scene shifts to preparations for battle and the final genocidal war between the Pandavas and the Kauravas. But until the end, Draupadi retains her firmness of purpose and defiant defense of dharma as she conceives it.

I have suggested that Draupadi achieved perfection in a further domain unknown to the pre-Freudian bards—that is, in the repression or denial of unacceptable feelings, a passionate personality was practicing rigorous self-censure. Yet at the same time, we know, from the regal authority with which she speaks, that Draupadi is fulfilled and serene. All her chores do not make her feel like Cinderella, downtrodden and tearful, largely because she lacks ego-involvement as we would conceive it. Draupadi does not put herself on the line, swallowing her pride each time she stoops to a task. The sum of her actions does not constitute her self. Her doings do not impinge on the true self: the essence of her being that dwells within and is at one with an aspect of the infinite Self of the universe.

By her actions, she is not submitting to, but affirming her place in the pattern of *karma,* deed and the result of deed. If she performs well, her actions will not be fetters, but the means toward a higher stage of being, a step closer to the true reality. Draupadi's karma, determined in previous lives, is to serve her five husbands with that nonpossessive devotion that is necessary for achieving *moksha,* liberation. The concept of woman's karma with regard to husband and family has varied little in two millennia. Sita and Draupadi are the exemplars, who channel their moral force and physical vitality into devotion to the husband. They are the perfection of *pati-vrata:* sacrifice (vrata) of self to one's lord and master (pati).

Of course, they are princesses, favored by the gods and generously endowed with the stuff of heroines. In a celebrated epic of the Tamil-speaking South, the pati-vrata is a young woman of a middle-class merchant family. The tale, *The Lay of the Anklet,* provides a vivid picture of daily life in a thriving commercial city in the third or fourth century C.E. It also demonstrates how Everywoman, by means of the perfection of wifely devotion, can transcend the limits of her suffering and attain her true power, releasing the shakti that dwells within her.

✦ *10* ✦

POWER AND CONTAINMENT

Kovalan and Kannaki are the young husband and wife in *The Lay of the Anklet*. Early in their marriage, Kovalan fell in love with a court dancer, Madavi. This infatuation led him to neglect wife and home and to spend everything on gifts for the dancer. Even Kannaki's personal jewelry has been liquidated for this purpose.

But a day comes when Kovalan, penniless and repentant, returns to his wife. She is "uncomplaining," even though Kovalan has fathered Madavi's child. The reunited couple decide to start life afresh and leave for the bustling city of Madurai. Their only possessions are Kannaki's two gold anklets set with precious stones. Kovalan takes one of them to the market to sell.

There he meets a dishonest court jeweler who has stolen a gold anklet from the queen's wardrobe. Detaining Kovalan on a pretext, the jeweler rushes to tell the king that he has caught the thief with the queen's missing anklet. The king sends his guards, who fall upon Kovalan, without allowing him to defend his innocence.

Learning that Kovalan has been slain, Kannaki faints away. But she recovers rapidly, galvanized by righteous anger, and goes out to the city to address the populace. "Chaste women of Madurai, listen to me!"[1]

The people are moved by the heartfelt grief of the beautiful widow—her "lovely dark-stained eyes," the "full moon of her face"—and by her passionate rhetoric.

Are there women here? Are there women
  who could bear such wrong
done to their wedded lords?
  Are there women here? Are there such women?

In rallying around Kannaki, the people of Madurai lay the blame directly on the king.

> Our King's straight sceptre is bent! . . .
> Lost is the glory of the King Over Kings . . .

They know that the king's dharma is to uphold righteousness; a king must safeguard social order, dispense divine justice. As Manu says, "If punishment is properly inflicted after due consideration, it makes all the people happy; but inflicted without consideration it destroys everything."

The people of Madurai are anxious and confused.

> A new and mighty goddess
> has come before us,
> in her hand a golden anklet!
> What can this mean?
>
> This woman afflicted and weeping . . .
> is as though filled with godhead!
> What can this mean?

A superhuman moral force is already felt to be emanating from Kannaki.

Meanwhile in the palace, the queen awakens from an ominous dream in which the king's scepter and royal umbrella fall, the sun is eclipsed, and a burning meteor crashes on the city. The queen has no sooner told her dream to the king than Kannaki presents herself, "filled with anger, boiling with rage," at the palace gate.

> My lord Kovalan came
> to Madurai to earn wealth,
> and today you have slain him
> as he sold my anklet.
>
> "Lady," said the king,
> "it is kingly justice
> to put to death
> an arrant thief."

But the second anklet is produced for comparison with the queen's, and Kovalan is shown to have been innocent. The effect on the king is dramatic.

> When he saw it the parasol fell from his head
>   and the sceptre trembled in his hand.
> "I am no king," he said,
>   "who have heeded the words of the goldsmith.
>
> "I am the thief. For the first time
>   I have failed to protect my people.
> Now may I die!"

And die he does. For a king must be godlike in his adherence to law and truth. As Rama demonstrated, a king must irreproachably preserve the dharma; he must, in Manu's words, "be beautiful in the sight of his subjects as is the moon in the eyes of mankind."

Kannaki, releasing divine retribution against the king, avenges her husband's death. But the wrong still rankles. Bitter and furious, she rushes into the street. Taking the populace, the sages, and the gods as witness, she rips her left breast from her body. With a curse, she flings her breast like the meteor in the queen's dream. Fire breaks out and is soon raging everywhere.

Not unlike Kali, Kannaki is in a frenzy of destruction. Only the intercession of the city's patron goddess convinces the young widow to withdraw her curse. Weak from her self-mutilation, she makes her way to a hill outside the city to die (being husbandless, she is already defective, no longer a valid woman). But she has sacrificed herself to obtain justice for her husband, and she is lifted into heaven for reunion with Kovalan.

What is the source of the intense heat released in the fire-bomb of Kannaki's breast? It is the accumulated force of her chastity, her submission, her suffering, her *vertu.*[2] Like Sita and Draupadi, Kannaki maintains a fierce allegiance to her husband, whose right to absolute constancy resides solely in the fact of *being* her husband. In popular festivals in South India and Sri Lanka, Kannaki is associated with Draupadi.

The two eloquent and forceful women are models of streedharma, devotion to their earthly lord. There is a strong Durga association as well. Kannaki, deified in local cults as a patron goddess of wifely loyalty, is endowed with Durga/Kali characteristics. She can both cause and cure epidemics; she is auspicious or inauspicious, depending on how her tremendous energy is spent.

To a certain degree, Everywoman is assumed potentially capable of calling upon such power. The literally world-shaking question is, what does she do with it? Shakti, as epitomized in the supreme goddess Parvati/Durga/Kali, is a volatile and dangerous force. When channeled, the energy works wonders; unchained, it wreaks mayhem. Thus, the Absolute Principle that orders our illusory world has established that the shakti be channeled, contained, and made responsive to the male. Far from being fissile tendencies or contradictory attributes of woman, shakti and streedharma ultimately fuse. In Kannaki, the white-hot flame of retributive justice ignites from the pure intensity of chaste devotion to her lord. Concentrated wifely subordination, with all the repression and suffering this implies, can burn like focused rays of sunlight through a glass. As such the threatening sexual energy of the female is tempered and deflected into service, nurture, and nonpossessive love. The power of shakti can be beneficial, "auspicious," safe, only when ritually contained—like the reactor's radioactive core in its massive concrete sheath.

To preserve the right order of things, goddess, epic heroine, and everyday wife all submit their powers to masculine control. Lakshmi, bestower of wealth, and Saraswati, purveyor of wisdom, provide models. Benign ladies without clear-cut personalities, they are tranquil consorts of their god-husbands. Durga/Kali is more erratic in her compliance; her flame is often at flashpoint. Benevolent and malevolent—her left hands hold weapons and inflict punishments, her right hands offer assurance and bestow blessings—she has her own being and transformative force, always on the verge of breaking out of bounds. The legends of this goddess and the lives of Sita, Draupadi, and Kannaki are dramas of power and containment; they reflect a recognition and a deep-seated fear of female power. Socialized to emulate these models, a woman may sense the presence of this force and know its accompanying burden of accountability.

Once upon a different time, an arranged marriage consolidated two wealthy Brahman families. A cultivated, well-educated daughter was wed to an only son. The boy was known to be a self-indulgent libertine; the girl "did not let personal considerations stand in the way."

After several months, the girl's parents received rumors of their daughter's misery. Not a sign came from the girl herself. "Silently enduring what the gods had put together as her karma, she had accepted that the spiritual comrade *must by her own goodness* overcome the evil in her mate. Such a woman was always considered the highest form of life in Hindu history."

Like Draupadi's pre-incarnation Nalayani, this young wife, trusting that her own penances could effect change, undertook a regime of fasting and prayer. Because she knew her role as emotional support and guide to her husband, she believed not only that she *could* reform him but also that it would be reprehensible if she failed in the endeavor. Her self-denial, piety, and hard labor would redeem them both.

After she had endured months of abuse and neglect, her father came and took her home. A concerned and enlightened parent, living in 1975 C.E., he proposed that the couple divorce. The girl's mother would not hear of it. The daughter must accomplish her "woman's role." Suffering was part of it; in fact, it increased the young wife's moral strength and quotient of virtue.

"The curious part of this," the writer comments, "is how deeply the average woman believes in her role of protector and sustainer. In cases without number, she is imbued with a strange, unconscious inner conviction that she is the source of strength, the unifier of . . . [all] the senses with which the human being is endowed."[3]

But there is nothing strange about this inner conviction. It is culturally determined: shakti compassed in streedharma; streedharma fueled by shakti. Credited with this inherent capacity and empowerment, the woman feels bound to deploy it and impelled to succeed. Otherwise, she may as well turn this force punitively on herself, rip out her breast, set herself on fire.

No woman can continuously perform at this level of expectation: culturally instilled, maternally reinforced, self-subscribed, and so thoroughly internalized as to be unconscious. Sixty years ago, a European woman married to an Indian witnessed how teenage Hindu brides settled into the families of the husbands they hardly knew.

> Two things were bound to happen. The greater a girl's innate but undeveloped capacity for individual choice, volition, and action—all tendencies sharply deprecated . . . by those who surround her—the deeper the sublimination of these qualities and the more intensely did she finally throw herself into forms of expression of exactly opposite characteristics: unquestioning obedience, total abnegation of self-will, tireless service, lack of initiative. The greater her frustrated urge to outer freedom and independence, the fuller her escape into spiritual submission.[4]

For the child-wife in India of the 1930s, Sita-like behavior was a way of coping with an inexorable real-life situation, accommodating to what one could not change. Remarkably, it remains the solution of some contemporary brides. Usha, the college-educated eldest daughter of a small nuclear family, was married into a joint-family, twenty-person household. She and her husband had a small bedroom that served as a general passageway and sitting area.

> Usha was almost a mental wreck for the first year of her marriage. She did not have the courage to tell her parents about her problems and make them unhappy. Time the great healer gradually brought about a change in her. She willed herself to accept community living without complaint. She is now of the opinion that "one must have a great capacity to give and share, listen and obey. . . . Maybe I was used to having more freedom and was over-pampered in my house. Probably this was the reason why I took time to adjust after marriage in my new home."[5]

Here, Usha's interviewers seem inclined to favor her change in attitude. As Indian women with a wary eye on disruptive modern influences, they appear to put the seal of approval on Usha's adjustment and apparent conversion. But there is a darker side to this coin. Confined to exile in an uncongenial household, where neither privacy nor intimacy is admitted, the sensitive bride can experience increasing depersonalization, even leading to suicide. The invasive sense of one's own nonexistence, perfected in death, is movingly portrayed in Anita Desai's novel, *Voices in the City*. Here, the diary notes of the last weeks in the life of Monisha, the young Calcutta wife who finally sets herself afire, have the lucidity and despair of the voice in the *Ariel* poems of Sylvia Plath.

And what role does the husband play in all of this? Sita's lord Rama and Draupadi's five husbands are also archetypes, caught up in cosmic responsibilities with their own dharma-crises to resolve. Obligations toward wives have very low priority. First come duties dictated by eternal law, then duties to caste, then to family of birth—father, mother, brothers, sisters. The mute acquiescence of the five husbands when Draupadi is dragged to the gaming hall and Rama's high-handed dismissal of Sita are ignominious to our way of thinking. But the heroes are not to be viewed in these terms. Just as the legendary knights of medieval Europe are paradigms of chivalry, the Vedic heroes incarnate warrior caste *noblesse;* in neither case do their domestic lives count.

As for everyday mortals, Manu's admonition resounds down the ages. "Though he be uncouth and prone to pleasure, though he have no good points at all, the virtuous wife should ever worship her lord as a god." Women who honor this dictum do reap rewards. But the reward can be quite ambiguous, as folk tales demonstrate. In one popular tale, a young man goes to great lengths to find himself the perfect woman, but some time after the marriage, he takes a mistress. Needless to say, the wife treats the other woman as a dear friend and continues serving her husband indefatigably. "In the end her husband was so enslaved by her goodness that he put the whole household in her charge, made her sole mistress of his life and person, and enjoyed the three aims of life—virtue, wealth and love."[6]

This stands in sharp contrast to the "happily ever after" of a Western folktale. Sensible, hard-working maidens like

Snow White and Cinderella always win a proper prince. What presumably happens to the heroines after "The End" does not include cheerfully serving the husband's mistress. Nor does the masterful husband proceed to abdicate his role, shrug off mundane responsibilities, and deliver himself, like a newborn babe, into the fond care of an all-gratifying goddess/mother/wife.

Stated in the extreme, it is a choice between the ineffectual, infantilized husband and the callous brute. Whether the epic heroes' behavior and Manu's exhortations reflect the realities of long ago, what concerns us is their contemporary actuality and the handicap this creates for both men and women.

The child-rearing practices of conventional Hindu families fix gender roles from the start. In a "traditional" home, the little girl is initiated as a toddler into household routines. She is given tasks and expected to comply with certain obligations. The male child is largely exempt from such demands. In terms of impulse control, attainment of skills, and observance of social norms, little is asked of him before the age of five or six. Indulged in his whims, passionately attended by women—mother, auntie, grandma—who may have few other gratifying emotional outlets, a boy may be programmed to become a narcissistic and ineffective adult. [7] As a male partner, he may be prone to dreamy irresponsibility or braggadocio, to alcoholic escapades or bursts of violence. Folklore renders this "acceptable." After all, men are just grown-up little boys, like the child-god Krishna, who rely on a mother to look after them. In everyday conversation, men are often alluded to in a good-humored, dismissive, or unconsciously condescending tone. They are not expected to be as resourceful and resilient as women; their capacities are measured on a different scale altogether. [8] This exaggerated concern for the needs of men's egos and the underestimation of their resources are so general that one can only conclude these attitudes suit most people's purposes.

When presented to a future father-in-law, a man may lie about his income, job prospects, or domestic arrangements. What does it matter? Flawed, failed, fatuous, he is pati parmeshwar, lord and husband, and that is that: the material one has to work with. A clever and tolerant wife will derive this-worldly satisfaction from getting around her husband; better yet, she may obtain credits in the next life for saving him from the consequences of his own moral or mental failings. All this is more satisfactory than open confrontation or revolt.

So the folk tales would have it. And a certain modern folk wisdom bears this out. The humorous short essays by women that appear regularly on the op-ed pages of major daily newspapers are revealing. In one, a housewife and teacher writes with humor of the "peak hour"—the early morning rush that begins when she jumps up quickly to suppress the alarm clock so that it will not "kindle husband's ire." Then, timing herself according to the three different wake-up schedules of her husband and two sons, she prepares three separate breakfast orders and cooks up two different lunchbox menus and two varieties of snack. She keeps everything warm but not too hot and manages somehow to get her sari on and grab a slice of bread to eat on the way out to catch her bus to work.

In another, the writer tells of a young woman whose family had answered an ad for a bride highly fluent in English. The prospective groom's contingent came to look her over. The group brought a friend, who admired the English books and magazines placed in view and conversed animatedly with the young lady. The groom-to-be said not a word, but the match was made. Later, the girl was asked why her in-laws had been so particular about English. She explained, "They have been so busy with their business interests that they never had the time to pick up any 'genteel' social habits. They discovered that for social mobility upwards, they need good English. What my husband needed most was a socially presentable wife."

Thus whether the circumstances are apparently grave or comic, women's inherent strengths are there to compensate for men's inadequacy—and to bolster men's authority. In time immemorial, the male gods gave over their weapons, implements, and energies to the goddess in willing abdication. Women have proudly borne the burden ever since.

◆ 11 ◆

ONLY A FEMALE

Housewife Found Charred to Death.
Suicide by Housewife.
Woman Burns Herself.
Three Housewives Die of Burns.

—items clipped from The Times of India,
October 6–16, 1987

In the parking lot of the five-star hotel, a *tamasha* is going on: a festive spectacle with costumes and music. All the passersby stop to gawk—shanty women on errands, porters and messengers, and the idle young men who materialize in twos and threes whenever anything is happening. I join them. There is no way to break through the fifers and drummers to do my prosaic errand of buying wholewheat bread at the hotel bakery.

Within minutes, about a hundred locals are enjoying the free entertainment. Then the arrival of two white Mercedes signals respectful falling back among the ranks. Several portly young men in dark suits step out, followed by glamorously dressed women. And, just like in the movies, there comes a man on horseback. The horse, a lackluster whitish stallion, is richly caparisoned. The rider, decked out like a maharajah, tries valiantly to look dignified under the huge turban perched on his head like a wedding cake. Lo, the conquering bridegroom comes.

The groom's processional arrival, a Vedic ceremony, is not

a daily sight in downtown Bombay. But the three-thousand-year-old ritual fits smoothly with the secular arrangements, the prewedding cocktail party and reception with a lavish buffet in a luxury hotel. There, in a secure place, the dowry may be displayed: the traditional *stridhan*—jewelry, silks, and gold, bestowed upon the bride by her parents and legally belonging to her; and for the new couple's happy home, household goods, the more high-tech and foreign-import the better.

Rare is the individual who contemplates marriage without dowry. Among very affluent and status-conscious families of some caste-communities, dowry can represent a considerable transfer of durable goods, real property, and cash. But the poorest and humblest family expects not only to furnish its daughter with dowry, if only a gold bangle, a new sari, a few hundred rupees, but also to realize a commensurate dowry for its son. The market value of an eligible male is figured on the basis of employment, financial expectations, education, looks, and his family's standing in a social hierarchy. The "floor bid" that the parents tacitly set may have to allow for obvious drawbacks, like his puny stature or a bevy of unmarried sisters. But one element operates in his favor. A man can choose his own time to come onto the market; he will be no less eligible at forty than at twenty-five. His family can arrange a visit to appraise the girl in question, but they are not obliged to close the deal. The girl who is rejected after literally being displayed feels humiliated, her family disgraced. Ensuing negotiations are more difficult, and the dowry demand climbs. Ultimately, no man—unemployed, deformed, or feeble-minded—is unmarriageable. A father of many daughters, crushed by dowry debts, may be ready to settle for anything male by the time the youngest girl comes up for marriage. What is the alternative? A sad spinster on his hands, a social and financial blight.

It is a no-exit situation. Families want to do what they perceive to be the right thing, and they want to be done right by. The girl's parents want to do right by their daughter—that is, fit her out handsomely with a dowry to show how highly they value her and to smooth her passage into the auspicious married state. The boy's parents want to do right by their son—that is, find the girl who will be the greatest asset for his happiness and ambitions. And the young women want to fulfill their duty toward the parents who have raised them and whose judgment and authority are beyond question.

Thus, the practice of dowry is firmly enmeshed in a system of cultural values. Nowadays, it is fashionable to raise an outcry about extortionate dowry demands and even to deplore the custom of dowry as such. But the deep biases of the society in which dowry is so tenaciously rooted are not often challenged, except by human rights activists and feminists. The ostentatious exchange of gifts, the tangible expression of goodwill toward the new couple, is only human: it blesses those who give and those who take.

A Dowry Prohibition Act has existed on paper since 1961. In 1984, an amendment was passed, ostensibly to put teeth in the law. Taking, demanding, or giving dowry is now a crime punishable by fine and/or imprisonment. Very few cases have so far been brought. A tiny but vocal nonconformist minority—progressives, gandhians, intellectuals—refuse to indulge in dowry in any of its disguises. But in certain communities, once austere and averse to displaying their wealth in lavish parties and wedding booty, ideas of status are now adapting themselves to the new horizons of consumption.

Emulation of flashy trendsetters and mimicry of successful superiors exist all down the scale, as lower-middle- and working-class families try to keep up with the times. Among families that have recently left the village for the city, as soon as their young men attain high school diplomas and steady jobs, the dowry demand climbs. The girls' families readily agree to pay the price for bridegrooms a cut above their stations. This trend is ironic: only a few short generations ago, bride-price, in the form of money or livestock, would have been offered by the groom's side to compensate the bride's family for the loss of labor and services her marriage would incur.

Both bride-price and dowry derive from considerations of the bride "on the hoof"—her shape, color, ease of handling, and her estimated lifetime output of goods and services. The logic can work both ways. One family may feel that their daughter—beautiful, cultivated, and sweet-tempered—

deserves a huge dowry. Their neighbor, whose daughter is equally meritorious, may deem these the very reasons to eliminate dowry altogether. But then they must find in-laws who feel the same way.

The original purpose and justification of dowry was to provide a cushion for the woman, propertyless because formerly women could not inherit land. Dowry was a compensation given to *her,* the jewelry hers to wear or to place in safe deposit in her own name. Legally, it would revert back to her in the event of divorce or annulment or upon her husband's death. In Muslim marriage, the *mehr,* the bride's portion, has exactly the same function.

Often, however, a bride's valuables are placed in security by her in-laws, who consider the dowry their affair, just as the new bride is now their dependent. Should the husband's family land in financial difficulty, there is no question but that the bride's goods will be tapped; she is left without resources. When she is comfortably integrated into her marital family or on terms of reciprocity with her husband, this may not become an issue. If, however, she is not well-accepted or well-viewed, then the in-laws may decide to put the screws on.

"When my marriage was first arranged, you all used to say that you do not want anything, and we knew that those who say this definitely want things," wrote Ranjana V., a young bride who left a written account of the harassment and humiliation she suffered before taking her life. [1] In recent years, the upsurge of postnuptial demands for showy goods, like television sets, motorcycles, stereos, has often accompanied maltreatment of the new bride with a view to putting pressure on her parents. Extreme and exceptional harassment results in dowry deaths—murders at the hands of husband and mother-in-law or self-murder following unbearable physical and psychological punishment. Observers in Delhi and Bombay, who have studied emergency hospital admissions, police records, death certificates, and newspaper accounts of suspicious home accidents claim that as many as three dowry-related deaths take place each day in these metropolises. Most of these are deaths by fire: kerosene and matches are standard kitchen items, whose use is subject to "accident." In greater Bombay, of women in the fifteen-to-forty-four age group who die "accidently," one in five succumbs to burns.[2]

Commentators in India tend to attribute the phenomenon to an avid frenzy for things, an epidemic of greed due in part to the pernicious influence of Western consumer culture. They see traditional values and constraints being flung aside for the illusory gains of the nouveau riche. But rapaciousness alone cannot account for the exorbitance of dowry demands, the meekness with which they are met, or the barbaric crimes that may ensue. One morning in February 1988, three sisters, aged twenty-two, twenty, and eighteen, hung themselves in their bedroom, to end their own humiliation and their father's desperate plight. Prospectors, one after another, had been coming to assess the eldest girl and demand a dowry that was twenty-five times the father's monthly income.[3] In 1985, one of the rare wife-murderers to be convicted and sentenced had already contracted a new wife and dowry, so certain were all concerned that he would be acquitted. In the summer of 1987, a young Muslim woman was "divorced" over the telephone. Unilateral divorce, *talaq*, pronounced by the husband, has been abolished in some Muslim countries, but it is still valid for Muslims in India. When the woman took legal steps to recover her mehr and valuables, her husband changed his mind, deciding that the telephoned talaq was not valid.

The cases are legion. The ones cited involved middle-income families with educated sons and daughters. In the urban slums, criminal atrocities against wives are an everyday matter. There is only one conclusion to draw: the female of the species is considered inferior, and any individual woman is eventually expendable.

"The birth of a girl, grant it elsewhere, here grant a son," says a prayer in a late Vedic text. Another verse reiterates: "Bring forth a male, bring forth a son. Another male shall follow him. The mother thou shalt be of sons, born and hereafter to be born."[4] The exclusive emphasis on sons and near-absence of reference to daughters is not confined to the brahmanic (priest-authored) texts. The songs and sayings of the common folk, often women, reflect similar sentiments. "As the turiyan leaf trembles with a gust of wind, my heart trembles at the thought that I may give birth to a daughter." Today, even self-styled modern families may resort to archaic magic to assure a male birth. It is common practice to celebrate by sounding the conch shell or the drum and to reward the midwife handsomely—only if the newborn is a boy. To be born female is seen as a misfortune for oneself and for one's family, possibly a punishment for wrong actions in a former life.

Women at all social levels seem to share this conviction. Some construction laborers who carry basketloads of bricks and mortar on their heads six days a week were undergoing regular Saturday night beatings at the hands of their husbands. A social worker asked them why this was so. "It's their right to drink and let off steam," one retorted. "They worked hard all week."

"And what about you? Didn't you work just as hard? Why don't you shout and hit him back?"

"Don't say that!" Startled expressions, hands fly up to tug sari borders close to their faces, cutting off further exchange with the social worker lady. How can a woman voice such a question?

But the self-image is not so different at the other extreme. In the early 1950s, a researcher interviewed Indian women graduate students in an Ivy League university. Her informants unanimously denied the existence of inhibitions or repression in India. They said, "There are no deviants among the girls. Boys do sometimes rebel. Never girls. But it is not subjugation. It is much more a feeling of security. We know that our parents know best."[5]

Parents know best, husband knows best, society knows best. Secular and forward-looking as Indian society claims it is striving to be, patriarchal attitudes and practices prevail. A Hindu male cannot die in peace if there is no son to accomplish his funeral rites. The departing soul is condemned to purgatory, with no hope of salvation. For the father of daughters, only a grandson can be an acceptable substitute. Today, daughters have equal inheritance rights under the civil code, but male heirs alone are considered the true preservers of family name and property. Adult sons work and earn and eventually assume the support of their parents, but a daughter's primary loyalties must necessarily shift to her husband's clan. Here, cultural traditions and practical realities reinforce one another.

Unquestionably, millions of Indian parents rejoice in the birth of a healthy female child, and many girls are their mother's or daddy's favorites. But too many families cannot afford the economic or psychological burden. "A third girl! I'll never be able to put enough aside for her dowry." "A third girl—he nearly divorced me after the second one!" In India today, state-of-the-art techniques can profitably resolve these age-old dilemmas.

"Abortions galore as sex tests flourish" reads a *Times of India* headline in April 1986. "Sex determination has become big business . . . as doctors offering amniocentesis and sex-preselection technique join hands with parents eager for male offspring, to kill thousands of female foetuses every year." One high turnover clinic posts unambiguously worded advertisements in ladies' compartments of commuter trains. Another invites, "Give birth to a child of your own choice; first time by successful scientific method."

A survey done in Bombay in 1986 made the stark revelation that of eight thousand fetuses aborted following sex-determination through amniocentesis *all but one* were female. This was worth lead editorials in the press. Said one, "Parents have argued that it is less expensive for them to abort the female foetus than to bear the expense of rearing a girl child and paying for her dowry. Thus for the criminally discriminatory practices of society, the girl child is condemned even before she is born."[6]

And if she is born and does survive, then the odds will not be in her favor. A study in a leading Delhi hospital showed that the mothers of boys breastfed for a longer term than did the mothers of girls, and they did not conceive again as quickly. At this same hospital, 65 percent of the pediatric patients were boys (that is, more boys were brought for treatment), and girl patients were admitted at more advanced stages of illness.[7] In another study of children with terminal illnesses, 64 percent of boys, as opposed to 48 percent of girls, had been brought to a hospital within twenty-four hours of showing symptoms. Of the children who had no professional medical care and eventually died, there were twice as many girls as boys.[8] Similar observations were made in studies done in two major teaching hospitals in Bombay.

Therefore, it is not surprising that a study done in the Punjab placed the death rate in the first five years of life at seventy-four per thousand girls and fifty per thousand boys. In the same state, a CARE team studied malnutrition levels among young rural children. A very large number were inadequately fed. Yet, classed by *degrees* of malnutrition—severe, moderate, and mild—the figures are striking. Of those deemed *severely* malnourished, more than two-thirds were girls, and less than one-third, boys. Among those mildly affected, the proportions were reversed. UNICEF data on children from birth to six years old, collected from West Bengal after the 1978 floods, show a similar trend. While distress was general, *severe* malnutrition was nearly twice as common among girls as boys.[9]

Since the mid-1970s, social scientists have been studying and analyzing such data from new perspectives.[10] Long-term field studies of daily human activity in rural villages have demonstrated the difference between the energy consumption patterns of men and women. The existing vital "calorie gap" results from both the larger amounts of energy women must expend in daily survival-related activities and the sex bias that determines what and when they eat.

As a result, India generates ill-nourished girls, frail young mothers, and the lowest female-male ratio in the world. India has 935 women for every 1,000 men (in Europe and North America, there are 1,050 women for every 1,000 men). Not only is this ratio low, even for non-Western, developing nations, but it is also *declining*. At the start of the century, life expectancy in India was abysmal—23.3 years for females, 22.6 years for males. In 1976–1977, lifespan had more than doubled—but women's life expectancy, 51.6 years, was a full year less than men's at 52.6 years (North American and European women can expect to live six years longer than men). Particularly revealing are the death rates in the age brackets up to thirty-five. In these growing, marrying, and child-bearing years, female mortality is substantially higher than male, in both urban and rural areas.

An adult literacy class in the corridor of a chawl, in the presence of children and spectators. PHOTOGRAPH COURTESY OF UNESCO/HUNNAR PUBLICITY.)

Woman at her chulha in a slum kitchen. Her basic minimum includes a basket, a bucket, a stainless steel tumbler, cooking pots, and on the ledge, a *boti*, mounted blade for cutting vegetables.
(PHOTOGRAPH COURTESY OF ILO (INTERNATIONAL LABOUR OFFICE).)

Mother and daughters manufacturing bidis at home. The woman cuts and shapes the tobacco leaf for the girls to roll and seal. The neatly arranged kitchen has a gas cooker and full range of stainless steel utensils. (PHOTOGRAPH COURTESY OF ILO/M. TRAJTENBERG.)

Construction laborers building somebody's dreamhouse. (PHOTOGRAPH COURTESY OF ILO.)

A construction worker loads on one last brick.
(PHOTOGRAPH COURTESY OF ILO.)

Woman and child paper salvage workers. (PHOTOGRAPH COURTESY OF ILO.)

A television interviewer prepares her questions at the studio. (PHOTOGRAPH COURTESY OF UNESCO/PAUL ALMASY.)

Sewing and tailoring at home for sale through a women's cooperative. (PHOTOGRAPH COURTESY OF ILO/M. TRAJTENBERG.)

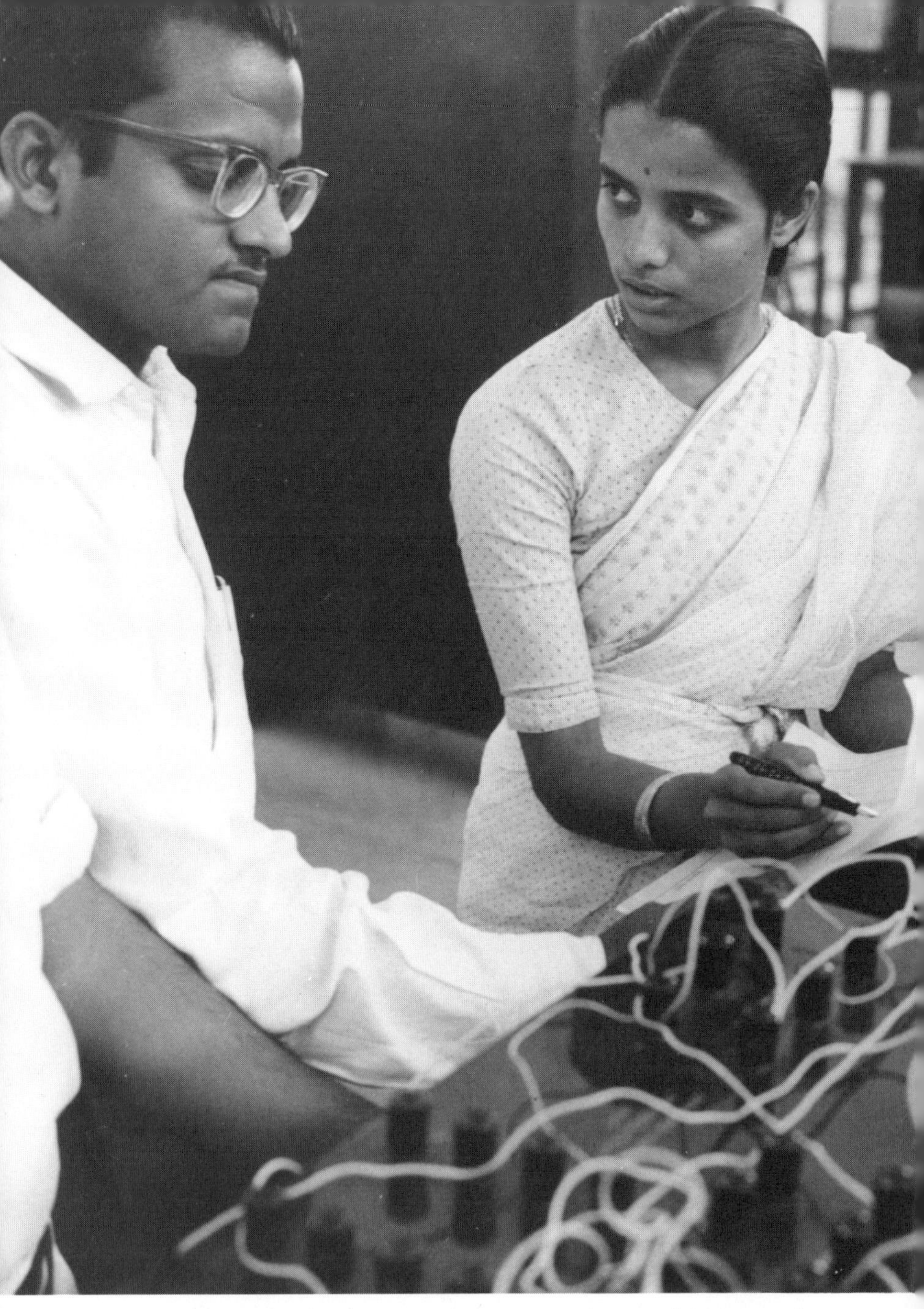

A laboratory assistant at a technology institute explains some electrical equipment to a student. (PHOTOGRAPH COURTESY OF UNESCO/PAUL ALMASY.)

A single newspaper item can bring it all home. Under the heading, "Death Sentence for Burning Wife," *The Times of India* (December 1, 1985) reports:

> The Rajasthan high court on Friday awarded capital punishment to one Jagdish, . . . for setting his wife, Chand, aflame on September 10, 1981. According to the dying declaration of Chand, she had been having a tussle with her husband and mother-in-law. Her daughter had been ill for a few days. She used to take the child to a doctor. Her husband and mother-in-law had objected to the expenditure on the treatment of a female child.
>
> On the day of the incident, Chand said she woke around 4 a.m. and went back to bed after taking glass of water. She had just gone to sleep when Jagdish poured kerosene and set her clothes afire.
>
> She cried for help and was taken to the hospital by some neighbours. She succumbed to her burns the following day.
>
> The Judges, Mr. Justice Lodha and Mr. Justice Sharma, said it was regrettable that a girl was considered a burden even after 37 years of independence. Crimes against women were among the cruellest, they observed.

Indeed. Crimes against women are more regularly reported as well—from grisly eye-witness accounts of the physical condition of tortured wives to earnest but ineffectual editorials in the press. Does this mean that the number of incidents, or only their newsworthiness, is mounting? Are more people concerned about a social scourge, or are journalists and other busybodies merely poking their noses in? Widows, despised and rejected, become nonpersons when their husbands die. Occasionally, a newly bereaved woman becomes *sati* by a more or less voluntary self-immolation on her husband's funeral pyre, despite strict laws against this practice. Indigent parents sell little girls into marriage or prostitution. All this takes place far more often than reported. These abuses with a very long history are assumed to be on the wane: that is, likely to die out as standards of living rise. But the gruesome deaths by fire, the murders or abetted suicides resulting from physical and mental cruelty, seem to point up a new type of social malaise, where enhanced economic prospects fan a sinister flame. Some suicides call to mind a desperate attempt by a latterday Sita, to protest her innocence and renounce this life. But most deaths have nothing to do with either choice or accident: they are murders accomplished without moral scruple and viewed by most of society with a complaisant eye.[11]

Vast numbers of ordinary people living in the pell-mell of urban India are in a permanent state of material distress. Along with it goes the psychological vulnerability that is aggravated when change, like a bulldozer, threatens familiar practices and relationships. To hold fast to as many of these as possible, while grabbing for the new goodies available, is a perilous feat. Structures so deeply rooted that they define the society—the caste system, for example—may be attacked from without by legislation, awareness campaigns, and new economic realities and challenged from within by individuals who revolt. Former untouchables may now be called Harijans—Gandhi's word for children of God—or scheduled castes, meaning citizens eligible for affirmative action in education and employment. They may convert to Islam or become neo-Buddhists to break out of the Hindu bind. But by and large they are looked upon and maintain a self-image as lowborn, destined for inequality. In the social and economic structure they deal with dirt: the women, as midwives, handle the excreta and may not touch the newborn child once it has been bathed; the men are butchers, tanners, trash collectors, and they cremate the dead.

Attitudes toward women and women's subjective image have a similar obduracy. In the summer of 1979, women activists who had gone to demonstrate outside a home where the daughter-in-law had been burnt to death were rebuffed by neighbors of the guilty family. The men jeered and made insulting remarks. The women were more virulent. The older women shouted, "What is the use of education when parents don't teach their daughters how to behave in their husband's house? Cursed be such education." "Nowadays, girls can't put up with the smallest thing." "Teach your daughters to bear everything patiently."

The young women shrugged. "What is it to do with us?" asked one. "The one who had to die has died, what's the use of making a noise about it?" said another.

The militants, though accustomed to hostility, were aghast at the malevolence on the faces of the women. As they withdrew, "a young woman smiled menacingly from her doorway: 'So you've come here to fight? Come along, we'll teach you a lesson. Go to hell!'" Her stream of abuse followed their retreating backs.[12]

How is one to look at this? What threat was posed, what taboos were challenged? What unacknowledged inner conflicts did the meddling militants stir up? The small community, a typical lower-middle-class subdivision in New Delhi, was closing ranks, not to defend a family, but to ward off "busybodies." Domestic violence is a family affair and thus sacrosanct, none of anybody's business. The police usually decline to intervene in a violent household on these grounds. As for the victim, consensus is rapidly reached about her "fault": she was cheeky or spoiled; she was lax in her duties. If nothing else, she was unfortunate, destined by fate for a particularly trying existence.

The distancing, the refusal of young wives to admit of any resemblance between the abused woman's circumstances and their own, appears pathological—holding the blinders on very tight indeed. The ferocity of the older women is more comprehensible or at least more familiar. The mean mother-in-law is a stock character in Indian folklore, both song and story. Matriarchs who have at last reached a dominant position in their household may view the seductive young wives of their sons as their natural enemies. Their stifled resentment of their narrow lives also comes out against their own daughters: why shouldn't she suffer as I suffered, as women suffer?[13]

The behavior of the younger women is more alarming. As I noted earlier, many women seem to take a positive pride in shouldering burdens, absorbing life's blows. In their innermost hearts lies the certitude: Whatever life has in store for us, *it is no better than we, being women, deserve* and no worse than what nature has endowed us with the power to bear. Shakti is there, the innate feminine force that is also the strength to endure suffering; streedharma is there, the dignity and exalted humility of the correct path.

That inner discipline and those powers of accommodation that make it possible to bear everything with Parvati's sweet dignity can, however, manifest themselves otherwise. Since the early 1970s, reinterpretation of so-called tradition, resistance, and outright refusal by women individually and in association have become facts of Indian society. Durga with her many arms and stratagems seems once more to be manifest.

A perceptive interpreter of Indian culture has stated that no other nation in the non-Western developing world has "such complex traditional institutions, the flaunting and open defiance of which constitutes such a high element of risk." Indian women are now taking these risks, as individuals, in small collectives, and through mass organizations. The same observer wrote, "In this century, Indian women have undergone a social revolution rather more far-reaching and radical than that of men. In fact this quiet revolution . . . is the most important element in the social changes which have occurred in modern India."[14]

The statement deserves attention. The first sentence is incontrovertibly true; the second, devoutly to be wished. "Quiet revolution" is a phrase that has its share of wishful thinking. Yet in the twenty years since these words were written, a groundswell has been growing. The image is not so much of a revolution as of local perturbations, from limited rumblings to eruptions that send out cracks over a vast landscape. In every domain, by their words and their actions, women are challenging the powers that be—venerable institutions, vested interests, conventional mentalities. And this is very much in keeping with tradition, a tradition exemplified by both figures of legend and mortal women historically close to our day. A first wave of women militants came out of their homes to take part in the national independence struggle earlier in this century. Gandhi mobilized their energies through nonviolent noncooperation, the paradoxical strength of the apparently weak. He claimed that he learned this technique from women.

Today, women are employing it ingeniously in their own liberation struggles throughout the land, as more and more find the power to say No.

Part Three

To Change Your Own Life

The rape victim, the battered woman is you, under different circumstances. You are as much a victim of the system as they, and you help maintain the system . . . when you look at these "atrocities" as issues that have nothing to do with your life. Rape and wife battering . . . are behavioral patterns integrally connected with the social values all of us live by. . . . To understand the interconnections between normal, everyday life and violent disruptions of it is a political necessity for women. The violent disruption reveals the nature of our normality. To try to end atrocities against women is also trying to change your own life.

—Ammu Abraham, Women's Centre

The local station of All-India Radio had asked Gita for a documentary on women. She called it "Winds of Change." Gita had run around Bombay taping women's words in half a dozen languages. She interviewed teachers and office workers as they boarded the trains at Churchgate, questioned a surgeon and a High Court judge, spoke with headload porters and street-hawkers—the whole gamut. As she sat reviewing the tapes at her dining table, she found one that was hopelessly garbled. Too bad—it had been the only record she had of a street demonstration against dowry.

Her housemaid, Sunita, who had been paying keen attention while she swept and dusted, gave her diffident, radiant smile. "If you like, I will bring my friends, and we will make it up."

"And to my surprise," Gita told me, "the *bustee* [slum] women produced an antidowry demonstration on the spot. They came out with rhymed chants and juicy slogans—they were vociferous!" Illiterate as they were, with no time in a dawn-to-dusk workday to listen to the radio or venture outside their neighborhood, they knew what was what.

A new awareness is growing among slum-dwelling women. Their recovered sense of self-worth and potential for group initiative take many forms. When one community of pavement hut dwellers learned that they were on the eviction list, the women, rather than passively awaiting the arrival of the demolition vans, organized themselves to search out alternative sites and design simple living structures to present to the authorities in charge of low-income housing assistance. Solidarity among the women was high. Those who went out for a day of surveying wasteland plots in far-flung areas of the city were replaced at their work by others. The initiative came to nothing: the municipal authorities refused to meet the women, and the demolition squad arrived on schedule. But the story made a five-column feature by a woman journalist in the Sunday newspaper supplement.

In another slum, an ad hoc vigil group formed to restrain violent husbands from beating their wives. One young wife had been reluctant to show disrespect and "give it back to him" as the group urged her to do. At last one evening she dared to grab her husband's arm and twist it hard. Drunk and unsteady, he lost his balance, fell, and passed out. The next day he was puzzled by his bruised and paining wrist. His wife enlightened him. "Every day the god strikes me, but this time the goddess struck you." The beatings ceased. This anecdote also found its way into a newspaper report on the emerging resistance of women.

Women who mutely accepted many years of brutal behavior are now broaching the subject—to a trusted employer, or a social worker, or someone in touch with associations that reach out to women in distress. Subhadra's maid's husband had become alcoholic and earned nothing to support the family. "If resentment was there, if consciousness was there ten years ago," Subhadra remarks, "it was so deeply internalized that she would never have come out and talked. Today, she defines it as a problem and asks me what she can do, what steps she can take to become more independent." The apathy born of exhaustion and lack of alternatives—the *inconceivability* of an alternative—is lifting, a little, here and there, not for everyone, but for more and more.

Such "consciousness raising" often involves starting from

scratch. Gender and intrafamily violence in general have only recently been acknowledged as grave and widespread social problems.[1] The "discovery" that wife-battering was going on at every social level gave rise in the late 1970s and early 1980s to investigative articles in the press and horrific accounts by witnesses and survivors. Harassment and abuse of women and the complacency—or complicity—with which authorities met it were beginning to raise hackles all over the country. It was not enough that the divorce laws were liberalized and that divorce was becoming a feasible alternative for more than just the Westernized elite. To seek divorce remains a very risky decision, in social and financial terms, for a lower-middle-class woman. She is likely to find herself isolated in a society that may no longer repudiate but cannot yet integrate her. The issue that needed to be aired went beyond recognizing marital discord and facilitating divorce. Wife-abuse, it was claimed, was only one consequence of unexamined attitudes and practices: oppression of women was woven into the very fabric of Indian society. Rekindled militancy and the mobilization around "women's issues" date roughly from 1975, the United Nations International Women's Year; they are related to the upsurge of women's movements worldwide. A few key events and the public protests they engendered have become reference dates in the contemporary history of Indian women's mobilization.

In 1977, a pregnant young woman was gang-raped in a slum in the Worli district of Bombay. The event unleashed a citywide protest for the first time. Slum women took part in public meetings and spoke openly about everyday sexual harassment. Several thousand women marched in protest against both rape and the slum conditions that were conducive to it. A campaign organization, Forum Against Rape, was formed; it later became Forum Against Oppression of Women.

In June 1979, in Delhi, a young woman named Tavinder died of burns after being doused in kerosene and set on fire by her husband's mother and sister. A neighbor, reading quietly on her balcony across the street, witnessed the murder. Her horror and indignation led her to instigate a protest, which swelled and multiplied. Crowds of women of all social classes demonstrated before the home of the killers and marched on the government offices to present a petition. A feminist organization, Stree Sangharsh (*stree*: woman or wife; *sangharsh*: movement, association) was born of this protest.

In 1980, two policemen who had been convicted of the rape of Mathura, a fifteen-year-old girl, in a police station, were acquitted on appeal to a higher court. Four law professors published an open letter of protest to the chief justice. This document sparked nationwide agitation, which forced the Supreme Court to review the case, and opened the way to legal reforms. Although the eventual results were meager, the Mathura case brought recognition to something that was beginning to coalesce into a women's movement. Its voice was *Manushi*, "a journal of women and society," whose inaugural issue in 1979 detailed the "common predicament" of all women and declared its mission to "reexamine all the questions . . . not only redefine ourselves, our role, our image—but also the kind of society we want to live in."

During this 1979–1980 period, the first academic women's studies unit came into being at the SNDT University in Bombay, and the Centre for Women's Development Studies was launched in Delhi. Evidently, women in India were responsive to the wave of militancy mounting in industrialized and developing nations. But they were also inspired by precedents in their own culture, the human rights and reform movements of the past. These movements had legally, though ineffectively, halted such medieval carryovers as child marriage and widow immolation, and they had written women's suffrage into the constitution of independent India. They had been the work of enlightened men, with support from sectors of the upper middle class. Even in the 1970s, the more affluent classes, by and large, produced workers for civil rights/women's rights; and the demarcation between helpers and helped was usually evident. The Worli and Mathura rape cases, the Tavinder murder, and the publicity and debate they stirred helped make more women conscious of the larger relevance of such dramas to their own and to every woman's life.

Subhadra Butalia, a leader of the Delhi march, recalls:

> We were not so many starting out, mainly university students and activists. But we were joined by passersby, and women who came out of their houses. By the time we reached our destination, the crowd was so big we could barely breathe in that June heat (~95° F). Then people began to bring cold water for us from their homes, and thank us for what we were doing. It was an authentic demonstration, not politically mounted, but spontaneous—the people raising their voice.

Recognition of a common oppression was beginning to seep through class barriers. Educated middle-class women who had never known physical violence marched alongside illiterate toiling women who experienced it daily. Women-specific issues were recognized as having wider social implications. "Every issue is a women's issue," "Human rights are women's rights," were not just slogans, but statements of fact. Urgent priorities like land conservation and resource management were found to be very much "women's issues."

The burgeoning of urban women's groups in the 1975–1985 decade was preceded and accompanied by sporadic but significant actions on the part of rural women who saw threats to their slim means of subsistence and the survival of their families. Agricultural laborers in Maharashtra mobilized to attack village liquor dens and break the wine pots in which their husbands were drowning the family earnings. Tribal women in the Himalayan foothills performed *satyagraha*, embracing the living trees that government contractors had been sent to fell. Small-town women marched while brandishing rolling pins against the corruption, hoarding, and profiteering that had sent food prices sky high. The smashed clay pots, *chipko* (hugging the trees), the clash of rolling pins on metal plates became pathmarks in the new landscape of protest.

Many committees and pressure groups that formed in the wake of a demonstration focused on single issues. Some collapsed after one battle. But many proliferated into today's active associations that tackle questions of rape, traffic in women, misuse of amniocentesis, testing of hormonal drugs on women, treatment of female prisoners, and all the myriad forms of oppression fostered by the family structure and codified in family law, with regard to marriage, divorce, maintenance, child custody, inheritance—in a traditional, patriarchal milieu, be it Muslim or Hindu.

What women were beginning to identify themselves as feminists and militants? Many had been students in the 1960s when agitation on campuses around the world also swept India. Some started off as classic Marxists, others as trade union organizers. There were research-oriented academics, lawyers, health professionals, journalists, filmmakers. Their personal conflicts and moments of decision are not unfamiliar.

Vibhuti Patel was a trade union worker. She recalls:

> We were aware of women-specific issues, but were concerned with working class slum-dwellers' and workers' rights. Slowly we realized that this was a way of relegating women's issues to the background. At the 1977 anti-rape demonstration in Bombay after the Worli incident, everyone focused on the lack of proper lighting in the slum, and the fact that the latrine, where the woman was going, was far from her hut. In all the outcry about electric supply and more latrines, no one mentioned that the threat of rape was constant, whatever the conditions. At that time, if there was a police atrocity against a woman, the leftist and human rights organizations would protest. But if a five-year-old girl was raped by her neighbor in the same slum, only feminists would pay attention.

She continues:

> With what agony we quit the unions. We knew railway workers, committed and courageous militants, who were very violent husbands and fathers. The union was fighting for higher wages and bonuses, but the families never saw it. The men took their salaries and went to the liquor dens. So what was the use? We proposed that the railway management give half the salary directly to the wives! So gradually the feminists took up family issues—non-class issues—for us, the real issues. We were immediately accused of having middle-class bias, and it was very difficult at first.

Vibhuti has been on the staff of the Women's Centre, a clearinghouse and general staging post for many campaigns and workshops in Bombay. The Centre runs local discussion groups and has also sponsored national conferences on violence and on women, religion, and culture, as well as regional meetings on the status of women in southeast Asia. The Centre has developed an orientation course for police officers assigned to investigate suspicious home accidents, as well as volunteer training programs for women who wish to help others in distress. It is one of several urban organizations whose volunteers intervene to help battered women flee home. Going in a phalanx to the victim's residence, at her request, they oversee her departure and help her recuperate her ration card and whatever jewelry and personal belongings she can muster. As much as possible temporary shelter, legal aid, and supportive counseling are also provided.

For initiatives of this kind to be visible and effective, networking with other agencies is crucial. Several years ago, ten women's organizations in Bombay set up Operation HELP, a round-the-clock monitoring of casualty cases of women admitted to one hospital after alleged domestic accidents. The hospital, located in a lower-middle-class and slum area, had the largest number of such cases reported in Bombay. Relays of volunteers arranged to accompany the police, hear all the statements, monitor the interactions between the victim's family, her in-laws, and the police, and remain present at the dying declaration if such occurred. In this way, opportunities for manipulation of evidence and outright bribery were diminished, and evidence for possible criminal charges was gathered first hand.

Full-time paid staff members of the Women's Centre generally have some professional background. But abused wives in the process of divorce or women summarily divorced by talaq and seeking shelter may at first come for help and then remain as resource people or full-time workers. While there are evident dissimilarities between the helpers and the helped, the "us and them" mentality is absent. No one is immune from injustice and humiliation or free from confused thinking. One worker recalled, "Recently we went to intervene in a divorce situation, to help the woman take back her dowry. She told us she had a son and a daughter, but she only wanted custody of the son. Something like that prompts us to examine our own attitudes towards our sons and daughters.

We made it a topic for one of our monthly meetings, where a mix of middle class and tenement women sit together, each listening to what the others have to say."

Saheli, a woman's resource center in Delhi, works in a similar spirit. Located beneath the thundering roar of a traffic flyover (overpass), the office is always open to women in crisis. A core of full-timers develops health information and civil rights campaigns. Functioning since 1981 as a collective with limited finances but high visibility (many hundreds of women in dire straits have made their way there), Saheli ("friend, companion") is continually reviewing its priorities and strategies. To mount ladders and daub muddy paint on advertising billboards showing half-naked women will stop traffic and attract attention, but in the end it may contribute to trivializing the issue of offensive display of women's bodies. To spend days in a courtroom in support of a legal battle that is doomed from the start is necessary but without immediate impact.

Saheli originated when a handful of women began to recognize each other at street demonstrations around issues of dowry and rape. These women felt the need for a place where women could walk in, sit, and talk; they also wanted a base where they could mobilize their energies more productively. The loan of a garage, contributions of chairs, tables, flyswatters, and fan; small cash donations from well-wishers to pay for electricity and telephone—and a resource center was born. Saheli operates on a shoestring, and its members have their share of ideological and personal differences. But the basic commitments are firm: to aid women in crisis, to raise questions, and to inform.

Awareness-raising goes on at different levels. In outreach programs for colleges, the discussions revolve around feminism, sexism, and sociopolitical aspects of oppression. For the uneducated slum woman, "we try," says Radha, "to tell her about her rights, about the laws, what she can demand, and what we can help her achieve. An illiterate woman rarely comes alone. Usually, a father or brother will come first to check us out. But by the fourth or fifth visit, she has the confidence to come by herself."

"They learn fast," Ranjula continues. "Just the other day,

two women turned up, who had formerly come to us for help. There'd been a fracas in their slum; the police had interfered, bashed up some women, and thrown the men into jail. These two women came to tell us, as a courtesy—and they made it clear that they didn't need us for anything—that they had managed to organize the women, march on the police station, and get most of the men released. They were confident and matter-of-fact."

Zeenat then recalls a middle-class woman who had had such a sheltered life that she was literally too timid to leave her house and cross the street. "Her first step out was to come visit Saheli. She went on to become an active volunteer in another organization."

In its short life, Saheli has assisted hundreds of women to quit intolerable home situations and begin to rebuild their lives. It has been instrumental in winning landmark cases in the courts, where it enjoys *locus standi* status. But there is a constant pull between operating as a crisis center and developing political or educational campaigns. "Street demonstrations," Ranjula explains, "are not the only or always the appropriate form of agitation. When we fight the experimental use on women of hormonal drugs banned in most countries, we have a well-researched information campaign directed towards pharmaceutical companies, government officials, the press. This is political work. A grounding is necessary, or else we are constantly fighting for one immediate demand after another."

Yet domestic violence is ever present. Any morning, a woman or her anguished father or brother may be waiting on the office doorstep. Shelters and rehabilitation facilities for battered women are few. Sometimes a Saheli worker will take in a woman who has nowhere else to go.

Knowing the usual conventions of an Indian home, I could not help posing the question: "Can you bring someone into your home just like that?" Ranjula didn't blink. "Of course. Otherwise, how is it our home? It's physically and emotionally exhausting to keep these people, that is true. But I wouldn't be able to get along with a husband who didn't accept it."

To sit around with the Sahelis in their trousers and

rumpled shirts, their short hair, their cigarettes, their uninhibited talk, is to feel right at home. This could be a drop-in counseling center in the Bronx or a storefront in Watts. "Sure, we are deviants, in the positive sense of the word," they affirm. "But when we have to deal with the police, we wear clean, fresh saris to the police station, and look very respectable. No point alienating them—we're unpopular enough with the police as it is."

Gutsiness, humor, and resilience are essential to organization work of this kind, where happy endings are few and purchased at a price. The women who seek help are at the end of their rope; their lives may be in peril. But there is always a likelihood of lost nerve and withdrawal by the assisted woman, for whom social displacement and isolation are finally more fearsome than the discomforts of home. Especially when children are involved, the pressure from family and from within oneself to return "for their sake" is powerful. It is one thing to be a faithless wife, but another to be an unnatural mother.

When a woman in crisis finds herself unable to carry through her decision to seek divorce, she cuts off communication with the support network and the stressful alternative it represents. Thus, one or two years of legal proceedings, vocational assistance, and emotional investment may be lost without a trace. The reaction is of course disappointment and irritation but no bitterness. At bottom, there is a resigned understanding. How many women are intact enough to leap irremediably into a space that society does not yet admit?

One major constraint is the lack of alternative housing—women's hostels, safe low-cost apartments, or board and lodging, particularly for women with children. Some of the more traditional welfare agencies that work with the very poor have begun to recognize the specific work necessary with respect to women. Feminist groups may fault the established charitable agencies for offering palliatives that maintain the status quo. Yet outlooks are evolving. At a workshop initiated by the Women's Centre and attended by professionals from twenty-five agencies, a Dominican nun who worked in a slum community revealed: "I have changed a lot in the course of my work. Young women tell me, 'I want to commit suicide, but I don't have the courage.' I have to tell them, 'Come and talk with me, we'll go for an outing, don't think of suicide.' But if I were in their position, I wouldn't want to live either. What I tell them is not how I feel."

Many of Bombay's social and relief work agencies, including some over a century old, were founded by upper-middle-class women, pioneers in their time. These were women whose husbands or fathers were educated liberals, active in business or public life. They were particularly concerned to abolish child marriage and promote female education. The women's goal was twofold: to uplift the destitute, and to create for themselves an acceptable way to emerge from the isolation and intellectual sterility of inner courtyards, to play a role in a restricted, but nevertheless outside, world. The "good works" were patronized by men, in the sense that no woman could become involved without the blessing of her menfolk. But they set a precedent: women themselves were effecting change; they were not simply the objects of men's good intentions.

The Indian independence movement from the early 1900s provided women, again mainly from the privileged sectors, with another legitimate avenue of expression and the beginnings of organization on a national scale. National goals and political agendas of course took priority over specific issues of women's rights and status. But from these origins a number of women's associations with large constituencies evolved. They do not cohere, however, as a women's lobby. Each one has its own political affinities or is simply the appendage (women's wing) of a political party. A long-time observer of the scene remarks: "All the political parties are using women's issues for their own interest. If it looks like a good way to embarrass the opposition or impress potential voters, a party will take up a women's issue. We in the autonomous women's groups will join a politically mounted demonstration when we feel that creating noise will do some good. But we are quite aware of their opportunism."

On the more local scene are the myriad clubs and associations for women only. The segregation of girls and boys in childhood, single-sex schools, and the separation of spheres in adult life favor the formation of *mahila mandals*, women's social clubs. The conventional mahila mandal is wed to traditional values. Members may meet for tea and chat or sponsor some charitable activity, but they take a dim view of female militancy. Still, women who have become involved in a controversial local issue may remain associated in a purposeful way, and the genteel ladies' club may evolve into a women's action group—which, while progressive, is not consciously feminist.

"Feminists" do not enjoy a very good press, and obsolete catchwords like "libbers" and "bra-burners" are still regularly trotted out. Columnists writing in the glossy magazines feel obliged to make a cursory review of the question before coming down firmly on the side of the "self-respecting feminine woman," against "man-hating," "hysterical ranting," "chauvinistic" females. When trying to locate a copy of the combative journal *Manushi*, I asked several acquaintances, all university-educated, married working women in their forties or fifties. All had heard of it; none had any intention of reading it. "Ask Sujata, she's a feminist," they said.

Yet, in the general press one finds some of the most striking evidence of evolving consciousness. The English-language dailies emulate Western papers in running weekend supplements, often crammed with advertisements in color and devoted to life-styles, cultural phenomena, and in-depth investigation of current events. The large majority of the articles are written by women who address topics of both general social concern—child labor, environmental damage, food adulteration—and so-called women's issues. In the Sunday *Hindustan Times* of October 18, 1987, for example, of twenty-one articles other than sports, ten were written by women, including three on the center-spread pages. There were four pieces on women's issues: "At the altar of patriarchy" and "Satisfying the male ego" were contributed by noted feminist iconoclasts. Female feature writers in metropolitan dailies in Bombay and Bangalore are outspoken and intentionally provocative. "Why is a wife's success construed as an affront to the husband's manhood (at worst) and wifely neglect (at best)?" asks one—and then tells why. "You have given birth to a hero," says another as she leads off a vigorous attack on the Vedic models that perpetuate the double standard and the devaluation of females.

This should not suggest that the Sunday supplements and the monthly feature pages are a ghetto for women journalists. The October 27, 1987, *Indian Express* (Bombay edition) carried a special section on science, technology, and medicine in which *all* the signed articles were written by women. The next day's front-page story on the battle of Jaffna (Sri Lanka) was bylined by two women who were in the first helicopter load of journalists allowed into the war zone.

As of 1987, six of the fourteen reporters at the Bombay office of the *Indian Express* were women. When three-fourths of the top applicants to *The Times of India* were women, the paper had no option but to hire a number of them. In 1990, there were about twenty female journalists in the Bombay bureau of the paper. Once hired, the women have to fight for the right to cover top stories, handle tough political beats, and work nights. They stick to their guns. A former assistant editor at the *Indian Express*, now an editor at *The Times of India*, told me, "When I introduced my column, 'The Other Half,' journalist friends warned me off, saying I'd be dubbed a feminist. Dubbed? I *am* a feminist. My staff were all women at the time. They were constantly taking up issues at the paper itself—protesting the choices of stories that appeared, the angles of reportage. None of us has suffered in her career."

A professional association, Women and Media, documents and analyzes negative and trivializing representations of women in the press and on television. Women and Media interacts with other watchdog organizations, civil liberties groups, research and documentation centers, and militant professional bodies like The Lawyers Collective. All these work within the system toward goals that, if obtained, would radically alter it.

But they are realists. "It's a long process," says the journalist.

Even if an increasing minority of working women in big cities are becoming more liberated, the majority have no economic independence, no conviction of their own worth, no accept-

> able social alternatives. They accept the way things are and learn some survival method. We can't fool ourselves that there will be rapid improvement given the economic conditions here. Yet, even taking a cynical approach, we should seize every opportunity, get the maximum we can out of it, and then see what the next step is.

The Sahelis agree: "We can't say, 'Nothing is possible til revolutionary change is brought about.' We have to fight now for the individual rights of women within families, and try to achieve something."

And a Women's Centre staffer reiterates: "Once upon a time we were leftists, working outside the conventional framework. But when you are committed to supporting women in distress, it can't be done. The woman has to find a solution within the system, within the existing structures."

Resource centers and support groups help. Free and fair discussion in the press and on television helps, as does the growing visibility of women who have achieved success in personal and professional life. But for the masses of women who cannot read and rarely leave the homesite/worksite where they earn their subsistence, the primordial task is to combat economic helplessness, the dependence on male relatives, male suppliers, male contractors, male creditors. In this mission, working women's cooperatives have made tremendous strides in the last decade. Members of these collectives gain an increment of economic self-reliance and sense of self-worth. What is more, they begin to experience the solidarity with other women that can loosen cultural constraints and defy the inhibitions of religion and class.

• 13 •

THE COLLECTIVE VENTURE

"Something new is happening to us."

—SEWA member

Our racy little Maruti sedan halts at an intersection. Gazing from the window on the passenger side, I see a scavenger woman making her way along the curb. Her sari is a length of rough cloth the same dirt-gray as the gunny sack she is steadying on her head with her right hand. The huge sack bulges with a good day's pickings. Tucked under her left armpit are assorted squares of corrugated board that she anchors against her thin body with her elbow. Two boards have just slipped out and are on the ground. Carefully she draws them toward her with her bare foot. Each piece is worth a few paise from the scrap dealer. But how to retrieve them when she has no hand free? She will have to hunker down and risk spilling some aluminum foil from the open mouth of the sack; she will have to squeeze everything tightly in her armpit and hoist herself to her feet with the gunnysack wobbling on her head. For the moment, she stands motionless, her toes marking her claim, as we sprint away in the giddy flash of traffic.

From my early childhood I remember the men who speared paper scraps along the Charles River Esplanade, using a long stick with a metal prong and a body-slung canvas sack. They did not stoop or soil their hands. I pictured the woman with a sack hung from a strap across her thin chest, and her hands free to sort and gather. Such a sack would be cheap enough for the trader to provide, to expedite her work and increase his profit. But here there is no relation of employer and employee. She plies her trade, ten hours a day, without appropriate tools. The dealer translates her haul into a few rupees, however many he decides: take it or leave it.

Fabric remnant stitcher, incense-stick roller, waste-paper vendor, handcart-puller—these are forms of gainful employment for poverty-level urban women. Most of these women toil on their own. Many are in the perpetual clutches of middlemen and moneylenders. A vegetable vendor borrows fifty rupees from a private moneylender to buy a supply of vegetables from a wholesaler. At the end of the day's business, she must return him fifty-five. A junksmith buys scrap metal from a dealer to make simple household articles. She hammers at the metal with tools so primitive that it takes twenty or thirty blows to cut one hole.

As individual workers, these women possess no voice. Organizing is the only hope of getting off the treadmill. In Ahmedabad and Bombay, historical and industrial conditions have been propitious for the emergence of working women's unions. The huge textile industries of the two cities employed thousands of women earlier in this century. From 1911 to 1931, women made up 18 percent of the work force in the Ahmedabad cotton mills. More recently, with the decline of the industry and modernization of the remaining mills, women have been shunted into ancillary activities, like remnant salvage and load carrying in the cloth market.

In the early 1970s, some women in these rude occupations began to protest their impossible working conditions. Their plight was brought to Ela Bhatt, a trade unionist, who conceived the idea of organizing women who are outside the purview of labor laws. The Self-Employed Women's Association, whose acronym, SEWA, means *service* in many Indian languages, is something of a godchild of Mahatma Gandhi. SEWA at first was the women's wing of the Textile Labour

Association (TLA). This union, whose principles were Gandhian and whose original members were largely untouchables, had emerged in 1920 from a dramatic confrontation unique in the annals of struggle between capital and labor. The daughter of the most prominent mill-owning family of Ahmedabad was the leader and champion of the textile workers, and Gandhi himself orchestrated the 1918 strike, his first triumphant experiment with nonviolent noncooperation.

SEWA rapidly evolved from an adjunct of the TLA to a full-fledged organization, whose objectives were often at odds with those of the male leadership. In 1981, Ela Bhatt was censured for acting too independently. For its public support of affirmative action policies that opened educational and employment opportunities to persons from scheduled castes, SEWA was expelled from the TLA. Since that time, as an autonomous registered union, SEWA has been a pioneer, organizing independent craft and trade groups under its umbrella. It identifies and trains grass-roots leadership and establishes both urban and rural income-generating cooperatives. It provides banking and credit facilities through an accredited cooperative bank that is associated with Women's World Banking. It has initiated minimal social security coverage: life insurance, maternity benefits, widowhood compensation, as well as legal aid, creche, and primary health care. SEWA lobbies for labor legislation that will recognize "self-employed" workers as mainstream, not marginal, pursues legal cases up to the Supreme Court, and carries its message to the ILO and other international forums.

SEWA has an impressive record. It is the creation of determined women, who stubbornly and systematically battle resistance from all quarters: the city administration and the police; owners and managers of goods and capital; right-thinking citizens contemptuous of backward-caste women; unconsenting male relatives of SEWA inductees.

The conflict between the fruit and vegetable vendors and the city of Ahmedabad illustrates SEWA women's capacity to keep plugging. A number of them sit and hawk produce in Manekchowk, the central marketplace, as women in their families have been doing for generations. By raising cash and establishing credit through the SEWA bank, these women liberated themselves from usurers and middlemen. Some learned in SEWA classes how to keep written accounts. But Manekchowk had become horrendously congested by cars, motorbikes, cycle rickshaws, handcarts, shoppers, and pedestrians. The constant police harassment was an occupational hazard for open-air vendors. Along with physical abuse and demands for bribes, the women were ticketed for traffic violations or arrested on trumped-up charges. Then the municipal anti-encroachment vans threatened to bump them out of the square and deprive them of their livelihood.

All attempts to obtain licenses or negotiate with the police commissioner failed. Letters were never answered. Eventually, the vendors staged a sit-in in their traditional places, with SEWA organizers standing beside them in peaceful defiance of police prohibitions. Such tactics are temporarily effective, in this city where Gandhi dwelt, especially when press photographers are present. But the struggle dragged on: the vendors were never able to establish legality, and the police commissioner was permanently "out" to SEWA callers.

After several years of this, SEWA filed a court case and retained a nationally prominent civil rights attorney, a woman. The Supreme Court declared a stay on encroachment action and ordered the municipality, the police, and SEWA to work out a compromise. SEWA proposed a number of solutions, including making Manekchowk a pedestrian zone. More than a year passed before the municipality would answer. More months passed before a meeting date was set. The lawyer for the municipality was eventually fined by the court for his delaying tactics.

The women finally agreed to accept places on the roof of the market—provided that a staircase, an elevator, a lavatory, and a protective shelter were constructed there. In a detailed article in *Manushi* a SEWA leader sums up the position after more than ten years of struggle: "The vendors are still in their old places, the stay order is still in effect and the municipality has yet to build the staircase and shelter. The police are still fining the vendors and SEWA's lawyer is still getting the fines invalidated."[1] Nonetheless, this total standoff is a victory of sorts.

To follow the saga month by month is to observe the many levels at which SEWA operates. At the grass roots, it nurtures workers' initiatives and acquaints them with ways to resist exploitation. It supplies the contacts and the logistic support. Street sweepers, for example, whose day-long rounds once brought them two or three rupees, are now organized in a cleaners' cooperative that services public and private institutions under regular contract. Paper salvagers have obtained exclusive access to the waste paper at government offices and printing presses, which they sell for recycling, in fierce competition with private traders. Cane and bamboo workers, who make baskets and household articles, have formed a coop; SEWA brought in the All India Handicrafts Board with a training program to upgrade their skills and diversify their production.

At the next level, SEWA intervenes with local and state bodies, confronts the police, and goes to court. At a third level, it conducts surveys and does research to propel issues of poor women's employment, public policy, and law into the national limelight. One direct result of this was the appointment in 1987 of the first nationwide fact-finding commission on self-employed women—official recognition of a national priority.

The organizational structure of SEWA reflects the heterogeneity of its membership. Of the twenty-five women on the executive committee, nineteen are representatives of the diverse trade groups. These grass-roots coordinators work directly with women from their own cultural milieu and local area, with whom they establish relations of confidence. Many SEWA members have never been inside the administrative building in central Ahmedabad. Among them are Muslims whose customs hold them close to home and Hindus from low or scheduled castes. Some have tribal or gypsy origins associated in the popular mind with swindling and theft. Most are illiterate, with harsh life histories—early marriage, frequent pregnancies, unstinting physical labor for day-today survival. Those who get ahead are likely to be scrappy, noisy, and persistent.

SEWA members refer to each other as *sister* (the word *ben* affixed to the woman's name). I asked two gracious young English-speaking staff members at SEWA headquarters what the class relations really were.

Bina said, "Ten years back there was some hostility. We would come to them, ask how are you and that sort of friendly question, and then start talking about their rights, and the strength that would come from alliance. They would think, 'Who is this memsahib? What can she know? Her work is to sit on a chair at a desk. What can she know about us?' "

Chitra interjected,

> In my case, their perception was correct. I had never really understood what these women were screaming about. I have a cooperative husband—right now he's home cooking lunch for the children. I've never had a problem of personal freedom. When I started working with them, I realized: this is it. These women really can't move.
>
> Over the years, with constant dialogue, and meetings at which we try to elicit their feelings about the directions the association should take, they have developed confidence and feel freer to relate to us. Those who get involved in running the association, who come up from the ranks, develop with SEWA, and don't feel inhibited by their limited education. They can accept that whatever our exterior looks like, inside we have feelings in common.

A working-class sister offers her testimony.[2] Bilquish was abandoned by her husband, who sold all her belongings and ran off with the money. She went to work sorting textile remnants while her mother looked after her two children. The traders paid very little and refused her demand for a raise. She then went to work in a printing factory, "jerking gasoline out of cloth. There I ruined my eyes. . . . I washed cement bags for a while, but then they got machinery to do it, and I wasn't needed any more." She says, "I have always tried to better myself. I don't mind working hard, or going to work hungry. But I must have enough to feed my children and my mother. . . . When I heard SEWA was beginning a small *khol* (quilt and bedcover) business, I went along. They needed a woman to sort *chindi* (textile remnants), so I sat down. Since then I have been with SEWA.

"SEWA can be a source of strength in the Muslim community. We are building a business controlled only by workers in which all of us draw salaries. SEWA has put my daughter in the municipal school and provided free books for her. I want my daughter to stand on her own feet and not be married off like I was."

She concludes: "In SEWA I have met many different people. I have spoken in public, which I had never done. I was very nervous, but I did it. Today I have grown from a sorter to assistant manager in our shop."

Many women who have come into their own in the association are ambitious and combative. Chandaben, from a backward caste and rural area, went into the used garment business at seventeen when she married a millworker and moved into town. She now has six grown children, all in the used clothing trade. Her history was typical—being scorned and cheated.[3] "We are not used to going to banks and the sahibs insult us. We sometimes manage to save some of our earnings, but we have nowhere to hide it in the house. Our husbands or sons find it and use it up."

Chandaben, an early advocate of a women's cooperative bank, is now on its board of directors. As she recalls, "We held a big meeting, at least two thousand women were there. I addressed the meeting for the first time. I have brought women to open savings accounts. Even now I collect their money every day and bring it to the bank. I bring women for loans and then collect the installments. I think the SEWA bank has come about largely due to my efforts."

Chandaben's swagger indicates SEWA's impact: a leap forward in attitudes and behavior. She is proud of her new experiences at SEWA headquarters, where she has met "many new types of people and talked to visitors from abroad." She notes, "I have learned to wear a sari [rather than her traditional more gypsylike attire] and how to speak like the *bens* [i.e., more educated sisters, "ladies"]. This has helped me a lot in my business because now when I go to the big houses to get clothes I can speak to them in their way."

Chandaben recalls that her husband was very suspicious of SEWA at first.

> But when he saw that it was just a society of women and that Elaben [Bhatt] was very respectable, he stopped being suspicious. Now he is very encouraging and often discusses with me the new ideas that I bring home from SEWA. My position within the family has changed. Before, if the food was not well cooked or the house was dirty, my husband and older menfolk would insult and scold me and even beat me. But now they see how much respect I have outside, how I lead our groups of women and address meetings. So in the house also they treat me with more respect and talk to me politely and not as an inferior. I have much self-respect now and I have to keep it up.
>
> My attitude has also changed in so many ways. Before, I used to quarrel all the time with my neighbors and relatives over small things, over children, over water, over animals, over spilling garbage. Now I see that these things are not worth quarreling over. I try to convince our neighborhood women not to quarrel over little things. I have become more tolerant.

Chandaben's observations are a revealing mix of traditional assumptions and brand-new insights. She defers to her husband's authority as head of family, whatever the actual power relations may be. She has understood that her indifference to everyday annoyances has to do with channeling her considerable energies into a vital and gratifying project. A fast learner, Chandaben may have an inflated sense of her own importance, but she is clearly a woman to be reckoned with.

The words "respect" and "respectable" crop up often in her discourse. Having one's own worth recognized by significant others in the home and community is as precious as any gains in income or salable skills. Identification with SEWA brings respectability. The association has interposed itself in the hierarchical structure to which Indians are responsive. Independent, differently conceived than other institutions, SEWA and the many SEWAs it has fostered in other regions have proved credible alternative economic organizations. SEWA's perceived legitimacy is bolstered by its antecedents; its respectability, by the elite element in its leadership, particularly in the person of Ela Bhatt. Honors, awards, and political recognition have been heaped upon this exemplary woman who adheres to her Gandhian principles and gets on with the work.

My conversation with SEWA staff members was interrupted by the sudden arrival of two men. One, in traditional kurta-pajama, looked very agitated; the other, in trousers and shirt, spoke briefly and went off. The worried man then told his tale. He was a vendor of crepe paper garlands, firecrackers, and holiday decor. Diwali, the festival of lights, was a few days off: in terms of his turnover, it was Christmas and the Fourth of July. Self-employed and unlicensed, he had been vending on the sidewalk; then the cops showed up, slapped a fine on him, and confiscated his wares. He panicked. A casual observer piled him into a cycle rickshaw and brought him to SEWA. Where else would he find womanly attentiveness and the womanly authority to get something done about it?

✦ ✦ ✦

From time to time, the whine of electric mixers penetrates the office where we sit, at the hub of the Annapurna Mahila Mandal. We have come through the two front rooms that are already inadequate for the multiple activities they house—loan disbursement and bank counter, sewing and tailoring classes with eternal black Singer machines, and the areas demarcated for weekly health checkups and legal counseling. We have taken off our shoes to wend a path among the women sitting on the floor of the large kitchen and preparing the catered food, Annapurna's essential activity. Opening the door to the file- and carton-crammed administrative office, we receive an unexpected boon: cool air.

We have traveled forty-five minutes in the jam-packed bus through Bombay's stickiest heat. But here, the room air conditioner has not been installed for human comfort, but for the well-being of the photocopier and compact computer that are on order. The printout list of Annapurna members is already catalogue size. Of the thousands of working women who benefit from group-based bank loans, few would be able to recognize her name in our alphabet, and many cannot write it in their own.

Things are moving fast at Annapurna, and if the plans for building a five-story center do not materialize, it will not be through any lack of vision or enterprise on the part of the membership. Like SEWA, Annapurna Mahila Mandal—Annapurna is the goddess of food—grew from an already existing base and has firm roots in the blue-collar districts of Bombay.

For decades, the Bombay textile mills have drawn job seekers from a radius of hundreds of miles. Mostly the men came alone. There was no housing for families, nor did it seem wise to remove wife and children from the safety of the village. Mill workers lived in grim tenements, six or eight to a room, working in shifts, sleeping in shifts. They had no means to prepare their meals and could not afford restaurants. But also living in the tenements were settled families who had ties to the same rural districts. The housewives had many mouths to feed. By providing daily board to a dozen or so mill workers, the women could earn enough to cover their family's food as well. A network of "lunch homes" grew up. The fresh chapatis and vegetable dishes that tasted like home helped ease the anomie of a workingman's existence.

The clients paid for their meals when they got their wages, at the end of the month. Without capital, the women had to purchase supplies on credit from local grocers. Illiterate and unaware of how interest rates function, each woman soon became bound in debt to a retailer who charged more than 100 percent interest.

The woman's typical workday began at five a.m. when she lined up for water at the standing tap in her courtyard. Then came shopping, processing, cooking, serving, and washing up—a repeated operation because the men, working in shifts, came for lunch and dinner at all hours. Aided perhaps by her daughters or other female members of the household, each woman operated a small canteen. They competed for clients, and if a man quit one lunch home without paying and signed up elsewhere, then the women took it out on each other, rather than on the defaulting man.

In 1973, the mill workers' union went on strike. For six weeks the men had no income. But the women went on feeding their customers, even at the cost of pawning their marriage jewelry or household possessions. The union did not consider these lunch-home women workers; if anything, they were viewed with hostility for claiming some of the men's pay.

Prema Purao, a veteran union activist and wife of a white-collar union leader, recognized the women's predicament. She decided to help them break out of the clutch of grocers and moneylenders and form a simple association in which, though laboring as individual units, they could find out their common interests and collective strength.

A few years earlier, several commercial banks had been nationalized and instructed to make unsecured small loans available at minimal rates to low-income borrowers on a group guarantee basis. After two years of effort a pilot group of women who would dare to apply for a thousand rupees each was identified, and this first application was pushed through the bank. The women's fears of banks and formal institutions of all kinds were fanned by the merchants and moneylenders, who warned that a bank loan would open the way to government inspection, high taxes, compulsory birth control.

Instead, a rapid, tangible amelioration followed for the pioneer group. The good news spread throughout the district. Annapurna Mandal became a registered society and trust. Loan groups were formed by neighborhoods, and bank officers came weekly to conduct the necessary transactions in situ. Within months, individual indebtedness decreased; mutuality and group consciousness grew. When a woman was ill or about to give birth, other members of her loan collective would aid or replace her. Default rate on loans was very low. And from shared financial responsibility developed the sharing of problems and ideas, as social and educational activities burgeoned around the new group identity of the women.

Still, the work days and working conditions were no less onerous. Another strike, which lasted a full year and resulted in massive layoffs, launched Annapurna's second stage in 1982–1983. The strike was a double blow to Annapurna women: husbands and sons lost their jobs, and lunch-home clients quit Bombay. Local Annapurna committees began identifying their neediest members and securing loans for them to start other kinds of small businesses. A large apartment was rented to serve as a center for vocational training in catering and in non-food-related trades. Contracts were established with public institutions that had inadequate or nonexistent canteens—for example, medical facilities and telecommunications centers—for meal delivery service. In some cases, women desperate to leave abusive husbands could be housed in the institutions where they ran a nighttime meal service.

New markets were waiting to be exploited. Bombay's upwardly mobile middle class has discovered fast food. Party-throwing Bombay wants snacks prepared to order and specialty items for festivals. Office-going Bombay subscribes to a lunch-tiffin service and pays monthly, in advance. At the Annapurna central kitchen, an informal professional atmosphere prevails. Groups of women cut, peel, and grind, cook and pack the lunches in individual stainless steel tiffin carriers. Then the delivery women pile into a jeep that drops them off and returns a little later to pick them up again. Consultant dietitians and nutritionists have been brought in to advise and train new participants. Basic commodities are purchased in bulk, and food-processing machinery and cold storage have been procured. Serious space limitations are now the major constraint on the evolution of the enterprise.

Other dilemmas have come with success. Teenage daughters of some of the original members are now coming onto the job market. These young women say, "You urged us to stay in school, and now we have our SSC [secondary school certificate] but there are no jobs. If we have to end up doing the same work as our mothers, why were we encouraged to go for education?"

These girls, schooled in the Marathi language, have gone further than most daughters of the working-class poor. But technical and trade schools are beyond their reach. They lack the open sesame: fluent English. Within the Annapurna organization, a one-year vocational diploma course has been developed, but there is no guarantee that these novices will find employment outside.

The veteran Annapurna women proudly display material improvements and evolved ideas. They work as hard as ever, but they now taste the fuits of their labor. They feel more self-reliant and know the pleasure of having ready cash to purchase what they please—an electric fan for the home, devotional objects, toys and clothes for grandchildren. Many have determined where their earnings will *not* go: they will not make lavish weddings for their children or comply with dowry.

Among the younger Annapurnas, the trend is toward later marriages and fewer babies. These women are candid about having to rely on their own capable hands and sharp wits. Although they have few illusions, they do subscribe to common misconceptions and superstitious beliefs. Repeated abortions or sterilization are considered preferable to male vasectomy. As everyone agrees, vasectomy can cause not only loss of virility but also loss of a man's vital force in general: he may become even more of a layabout than he already is. As one woman put it bluntly, "At least they are good for something—with that operation, they'd be good for nothing at all!"

◆ ◆ ◆

Lunch is brought from the kitchen, and we all get a chance to sample the Annapurna fare. There are the airy golden wholewheat puffs called puris, dal (lentils), potato chop, vegetable sabji, spiced yoghurt, and a wickedly hot-looking pickle. An assortment of very sweet sweets follows and milky tea. Besides myself, there are an Indian journalist, the representative of a funding agency from Delhi, Annapurna's male accountant and legal counsel, and a Christian gentleman from Connecticut. He is a fish-farming expert, here on a voluntary mission to help Annapurna try out an income-generating project of shrimp culture.

The conversation is lively. Prema recounts how a group of Annapurna vegetable vendors outfoxed the policemen who'd been helping themselves to the choicest wares. Rajay, the young CPA, describes how the more capable women rise from the ranks, overcoming jealousies and rivalries to become members of the executive committee. His pride in the organization glows on his face: he speaks always of *we*.

The no-nonsense woman from Delhi reports on the weekend she has just spent at the Bombay home of her niece, a full-time housewife. "Saturday her husband rented twelve hours' worth of videotapes. He and the kids sat down and watched five films. The whole weekend they did nothing else. If my niece hadn't cooked and served and cleared up for them, they'd have complained that they were being neglected. That's what being neglected is about, when men complain!"

The evocation of middle-class indulgence makes us shift in our seats—we are all middle class here. None of us will ever have to roll out chapatis from dawn to dark, seven days a week. Nor is it likely that an Annapurna woman will ever know the leisure of two consecutive days with only a bit of cooking and serving to do for a husband and children glued to a TV set. We take facile comfort in the existence of organizations like Annapurna and SEWA. Their impressive achievements are not without ambiguities. Some Indian leftists and feminists point out that while such associations have raised the members' economic level, they have given little relief from long, monotonous hours and oppressive conditions—and no real alternatives have emerged. "The productive activity is cooking—merely an extension of what they'd be doing anyway."[4]

Not only are traditional roles and behaviors reinforced, but hierarchical relations also seem ineluctable. Exceptional women head these organizations.[5] They come from supportive, enlightened families and possess a personal charisma. Their mode of operation involves some degree of tutelage. Willy-nilly, they are often held in reverential esteem. Still, their guidance and example inspire other women to try out new roles and values. They are not preparing the revolution, but pushing at the limits of the feasible, attempting to encourage personal initiative and build confidence.

For example, Annapurna women who have saved a sufficient sum organize trips, making a study-tour of the Hindu temples in the south or of the capital city of New Delhi and the nearby Taj Mahal. It is the first time these women will have traveled any distance without accompanying children or family. It is an adventure and a powerful learning experience.

Fifty-three women went on a pilgrimage to the holy city of

Benares. There, Hindus take purifying baths in the Ganges and make offerings to the gods in the temples and shrines. But Benares is also a business, and one does not walk into a holy place just like that—especially if one is female.

Prema, who knows how to tell a story, recounts how the group was set upon by *pandas*, the Brahman guides whose function is to see to the priestly and practical needs of pilgrims, for a fee. Prema suggested that each woman in the group put in five rupees for the collective purchase of the ritual necessities: sandalwood paste, sweets, flowers. She proceeded to negotiate with the pandas about their fee for reciting the Sanskrit vows. Expecting to bargain with each customer separately, the pandas balked at performing their services. In the heated discussion that followed, questions were raised: some of the women must be widows, or menstruating, and would thus require different arrangements. But Prema would hear none of this.

"You are Brahmans, and I am a Brahman's daughter," she said. "Please tell me where it is written in the Vedas that a woman cannot make *puja* [worship] directly, that a widow or a menstruating woman is inauspicious." The pandas tried a different tack, calling her Mother, deferring to her rank, fawning but insistent. Sanctimoniously, they invoked their own piety. Helping people to worship properly was their hereditary duty and their livelihood.

Prema scrutinized the balls of rice, called *pinda*, that pilgrims buy to be symbolically offered to their ancestors in the course of worship. They had a dubious look. She picked one up. Paah! It smelled putrid. It had been made and remade many times from the same rice, instead of freshly cooked grains. The pandas were cheating on a cosmic scale, proferring something ritually unclean, an insult to gods and ancestors.

As she recalled the ignominious retreat of the Brahmans, Prema's round, kindly face beamed a mischievous smile. For the Annapurna women, travel must be broadening indeed in such company. And new possibilities are taken quite in stride. A group who went by train to the far south to visit ancient temples came back well satisfied, already making plans for a future excursion.

"Only next time," they confided, "we are going by plane."

◆ 14 ◆

CARELESS DAUGHTERS

Rise up, ye women that are at ease!
Hear my voice, ye careless daughters!

—Isaiah 32:9

Tara's driver came for us at four-thirty p.m. I was going to tea with my friend Sheela and her great-aunt to meet Tara, Sheela's new cousin by marriage. Because it would be high tea in someone's home, in the company of an august elderly lady, I wore a sari. The three of us, all starched cotton billows, squeezed into the back seat of the Ambassador, the stout Indian automobile designed for durability, not comfort. "Why she didn't send the Mercedes," the great-aunt muttered to herself.

We were handed smoothly from driver to doorman to elevator attendant to the uniformed maid who opened the massive carved mahogany door of the tenth-floor apartment. We stepped along a plant-lined, marble-paved entry hall hung with framed and illuminated Moghul miniatures. Reggae rock music was coming out of the walls.

"Lovely to see you!" A statuesque woman came forward, her dark hair piled in a high topknot like a Bodhisattva sculpture. She was wearing a rumpled, impeccably white cowl-neck shirt and cotton trousers, export manufacturers' seconds that hawkers sell on the sidewalk outside the museum. She'd got it, she told me later, for thirty rupees (less than two dollars); she'd hard-bargained him down. For accessories, she wore half a pound of solid gold jewelry: heavy choker, broad bangles and ear clips of fretted two-tone gold, and two similarly patterned rings on her right hand. Her wedding ring was four bands of small matched diamonds. With a pearl-polished fingernail she switched off the stereo. Her other arm held her four-month-old daughter.

For the whole length of the visit, hovered over by cook, maid, and nanny and punctuated by arrivals of various delivery boys, Tara did not put the baby down. She installed herself next to her husband's Aunty and attended assiduously to the eldest guest, while Sheela and I took a stroll around the vast living room. The triple picture window commanded a wide-screen view of other luxury apartment buildings, construction workers' shanties, a washermen's colony, the bay, and the open sea. The room was furnished with antiques and bronzes, the walls a gallery of ancient and contemporary Indian art.

After a few minutes, we were called into the dining room and seated at one end of the formally laid table. Tara settled the baby on her lap and supervised the serving of tea and platefuls of mini-kebabs, vegetable fritters, chickpeas in sauce, chutneys, fruit pudding, milk sweets, cakes. We fell to, using the heavy sterling silver service. Tara fed herself with the fingers of her right hand, in the traditional manner. In her cultured British accent, she expressed her regret that her stepchildren were not at home—gone to the club for swimming and tennis. She spoke feelingly of the unhealthy materialism of the other children in their exclusive school, the loss of traditions, the decline of values. She alluded to her travels to Paris and New York and assured us that "Americans are not aware of anything outside their own suburb." We got up from the table to resettle in the living room and digest for a while. Tara remarked that in this unbearably hot weather she fortunately did not ever have to step out of the apartment.

Not even in the air-conditioned Mercedes, I thought. I knew that Viraj, the business magnate whom she married just a year ago, was not quite as fabulously rich as her former husband, but certainly a safer investment than the romantic polo player with whom she had enjoyed the escapade that finished off her first marriage. I thought of one or two of my own friends who walk a fine line and thrive on provocation. Tara won hands down.

The glossy Bombay magazines call them the *glitterati*—moneyed, arrogant women and men for whom there are no limits. Evidently, one has a sense of outrage. The coarse-featured, heavily made-up, obese woman in a chiffon sari waddling down the steps of the Taj Mahal Hotel is repulsive to look at. Her abdomen and flabby sides hang in dewlaps: the sari was not meant to wrap so much meat. Moral revulsion follows closely on the physical. The abject wretchedness all around makes the contemptuous indifference of the super-rich more reprehensible. The view from their protected eyrie is too squalid; the bitter toil of the many, omnipresent.

A magazine reports an exhibition-sale of arty original T-shirts painted in one-of-a-kind designs, sold out in one hour at 2,500 rupees *each*. Rock-and-roll fashion shows are jammed; lines form at glamorous restaurants that coyly hint at Western naughtiness—"Ménage à Trois" features "small-is-beautiful designer meals, composed of an intriguing selection of befores and afters."

Most Bombay-based magazines, even those aimed at the swinging hedonist, carry a somber article or two on conditions affecting the vast majority. But the inaugural issue of a publication launched in 1987 and purporting to "tell all" about what goes on in the megacity, frankly dispensed with any token piece on dreary topics like slums, pollution, or civic irresponsibility. That is all simply part of the folklore, the tough charm that adds spice to living here. Terrible, yes, but what to do? One is not a social worker.

Snide articles and letters lampooned the celebrated actress who joined a hunger strike of slum dwellers whose huts had been razed and no alternative site proposed by the local government. "Let her settle them in her compound at Juhu [the suburb of the stars]," the upper middle class sniffed and dismissed the topic. The problem would have gone away, they felt, if the actress had not turned it into a publicity stunt.

For the outsider, the inevitable sense of outrage is like a shot of adrenalin at first. It can go stale and eventually resolve into a self-protective irony. The problems *are* enormous, and the native aptitude for denial and dissociation makes it possible to keep from being overwhelmed. If you lived here, what would you do?

For some, the work of mother, wife, and home manager is not only full-time, but it has also taken on new and surprising dimensions. A Bombay reader wrote to a women's column in *The Times of India:*

> My mother had to be just "mother." She was there to tend to my creature comforts and worry about my well-being. I have to be a friend, guide and critic to my children—meet their teachers, take them for swimming lessons; mediate between them and their papa about long hair and faded jeans. I must be game to go on picnics, struggling into my too tight jeans; cook for an army of my son's friends who decide to stay and watch a movie on video; stand in at rehearsals of jam sessions, and succumb to entreaties to be a darling mom and make French fries after a hard day's work.

Add a salaried job or profession to the program—more balls to juggle and the added guilt about giving short shrift to one's roles as mother and homemaker. Women with professions may mask their enthusiasm and take care not to manifest a strong commitment to their "outside" work. They are, after all, the product of an education that has put a premium on docility and performance and systematically discouraged original thinking and personal initiative. The school uniforms that are still worn, regulated down to the very color of the elastic binding one's braids, are emblematic of the uniformity sought. Great chunks of biology are learned by rote, with all the Latin nomenclature and perfectly copied diagrams, and regurgitated in frequent exams. Victorian attitudes prevail. The "home science" teacher cautions young ladies not to touch any part of their person while preparing food. The poetry teacher marks the beat as the class belts out in unison "The *boy* stood *on* the *bur*-ning *deck.*" Bright girls work faithfully and earn high marks; then are admitted to science faculties where they keep at it, living in single cells in women's hostels. Meanwhile, their families begin putting out feelers for commensurate mates.

A survey of postgraduate science degree holders made in the late 1970s examined these women's motivation for self-growth and professional development and their views of their role as scientific workers in relation to other roles.[1] Forty percent of the women were unmarried. Most of those who were voluntarily not employed were married with young children. They placed a high value on staying at home, even when there were domestic helpers or grandparents in the household. One top graduate felt that "a woman should work only if her husband does not earn enough or if her family needs money for her marriage expenses."

All those who were not working agreed that scientific training encouraged critical awareness and claimed they kept up with their field. Yet without exception, they believed in destiny (karma). Many observed fasts, vows, or ritual taboos. Science, they felt, may explain natural events, but there is a power of destiny beyond human comprehension and control.

The women surveyed had received master's or doctoral degrees in the late 1960s or early 1970s. Younger women, born at least a decade later, place higher priority on both professional and personal development. Most of them come from educated and supportive families. Many have been affected by the women's movement.

Yet, to survive in a profession where men make the rules, a woman may lean over backwards to emulate male colleagues and dissociate herself from anything that smacks of "women's problems." No less a model than Indira Gandhi did the same. Indira, as the story goes, took it as a compliment to be dubbed "the only man in her cabinet."

Once established in a position of relative authority, a woman can be brutal in her way of exercising it. Physicians who run sterilization "camps"—all-day cut-and-tie marathons with quotas to meet—work with a chilling disregard for their patients as individuals. In a court case brought by newly recruited young hospital nurses who had been compelled illegally to undergo virginity tests, it emerged that the procedure used, the most painful and invasive method, had been imposed by a woman doctor.[2]

Such individuals are not apt to ally themselves with women colleagues or women's causes. Their interests lie in maintaining the status quo and their own privileges in it. This is the case for many of the women who hold political office. Those who have been tapped to run for parliament by the male-dominated political parties are very often wives, widows, or daughters-in-law of powerful male politicians. A few women politicians on the left identify themselves with women's protest and actively campaign, rather than simply propagating the party line. But the rest are largely from upper-caste land-owning or industrialist families; some are descendants of the old princely houses. Few have a political program or perspective, and their allegiances are clear. Politics is just an extension of family business.

And then, there are the mavericks—lucid, principled, independent, the very antithesis of a bourgeoise maharani like Tara, though generally issuing from the same privileged class. They are true originals, whose only resemblance to one another is in the passionate conviction each brings to her work and the relative simplicity in which each one lives.

One who has a redoubtable reputation is Madhu Kishwar. "I'm a mule, born to be a mule in a human body," says the founder and editor of the path-breaking journal *Manushi*. Strongly opposed to state intervention even in the name of social reform, Madhu feels that the purpose of any social action is to create space for more humane norms for dealing with people in general, and women in particular. Highly articulate and quick to speak her mind, Madhu, who has been a human rights activist since her student days, refuses all labels, including that of feminist. She is wary of theorizing and romanticizing about a struggle that proceeds through sheer drudgery and repeated setbacks. "It's an epochal struggle, but it has to be done. Our existence, *Manushi*'s existence are a challenge—we are living that challenge every day."

Another is Niloufer Bhagwat, a firebrand attorney whose practice thrives in Bombay. Her husband is posted in New Delhi. This makes for a commuting marriage; one teenage child stays with each parent. Niloufer feels that only since the mid-1980s have women's issues come to the fore. "The failure of ranking women in the political parties was total. Their attitude was superficial, patronizing—as if these were charity issues. No one was paying attention to the magnitude of women's contribution to the basic economic unit of society, the household."

Access to legal aid in Bombay has greatly improved, Niloufer feels, but a woman who seeks divorce is in a very shaky state. She has no economic security. She is terrified about going to a court of law against her own husband. "Many of the women who come to me are suffering from depression, and no wonder. The whole ethos is that your life begins and ends with marriage. It doesn't matter if you don't know what it is to step out of your home and attend a meeting, if you have not known even twenty-four hours of happiness. Your existence is meant for your husband and children—you have no right to exist as an individual."

Niloufer views the court proceedings as an opportunity for a woman to see how a branch of the state functions vis-à-vis her own life. "I tell my client, 'You and I are confronting not only your husband who is a product of this society, but also the state, which thinks that we should not be coming here to air our woes.' The woman must be led to question: What does this institution represent? Who appoints the judge? What are his biases? This must be an educational experience for the client. An attorney should never take the attitude that this is a charitable exercise."

A senior woman colleague had recently appeared on behalf of a Parsi woman who asked, as part of her divorce settlement, that the apartment where she had lived with her husband be divided in two, with separate entries. Otherwise she would be on the street. The older lawyer hesitated. "Where is the precedent for this?" she asked.

"We are to evolve the precedents," Niloufer replied. "That is what we are here for. Our part of the struggle, in the legal profession, is to create the concepts, establish the precedents."

Niloufer's doctoral degree is in administrative jurisprudence. Her additional caseload as a women's rights advocate is exhausting. After a period of ill health in 1987, she considered curtailing this activity for a while. But a letter from her sixteen-year-old son rallied her. "Ma," he wrote, "don't be a dormant volcano."

◆ ◆ ◆

"My husband is an executive who works in five-star hotels. I work on five-star construction sites."

So speaks Indu Balagopal, with her eloquent smile. We have just stepped out of a teeming creche, a slapped together brick cabin roofed with metal sheeting. "The five- and six-year-olds here are old hands at Bombay life," Indu remarks. "Video culture, alcohol, everything. A foreign visitor doesn't cause many heads to turn. But if I took you to one of our sites in the suburbs, where the workers are raw recruits from the village—the children would start to cry at the sight of you."

Indu, a physician, is the prime mover of Mobile Creches in Bombay (described in Chapter 5). But she herself attributes the originality and strength of the operation to its staff of teachers and creche workers, who are drawn from the lower middle class. These women may have only a primary school education and no work experience. They come from modest, traditionally oriented families, and they need an income. A one-year training course, in the classroom and onsite, develops their competencies. They produce the teaching materials and invent the stories, songs, and games. Ingeniously they arrange the spaces of the creche as they have learned to do in the cramped all-purpose rooms in which their own families live.

To transform women who had been taught by the rule into innovative and permissive teachers has meant undoing lifelong habits of timidity and deference. Indu recalls, "At staff meetings, they used to open their notebooks and get ready to write. I said, 'I am not going to say anything you can write down and follow. You think about the question and make some suggestions.' They insisted, 'Didi [Big Sister], please tell us what to do.' It took a lot out of us, but eventually they got there. Now it is so decentralized that I don't initiate discussions or take decisions at meetings. It may be that so-and-so has come to work late ten times. She has domestic problems. Some of the staff are punitive toward her, some are more tolerant. They have to develop a consistent policy and follow it through."

"Sometimes I think this is making them schizophrenic," Indu says ruefully. "A group of creche workers told me, 'Now we understand. You forced us to learn to think for ourselves. Here we talk, argue, take decisions. But at home if we speak up like that, we are told, 'Who do you think you are?' "

Many staff workers share their homes with dominating mothers-in-law. One woman found that in her absence her own baby was being fed rice water. She asked her mother-in-law to give the child milk. "Don't act smart," retorted the older woman. "I've raised many children on rice water. If you don't like the way I look after your baby, take it with you to the creche."

And she did. It was a courageous step for the young woman, not only to defy hierarchical authority, but also to disregard social taboos and let her child mix with the motley crew in the creche.

Another worker, mother of two girls, was pregnant. The family was praying for a boy—if not this time, then the next. But the woman informed her husband that she was going to have herself sterilized after the delivery, whatever the outcome.

"How they have blossomed out, and how difficult it was for them at every step," Indu recalls. "At the start, I asked: 'If the children are dirty and unkempt, will you be able to teach?' Most of them said, 'No.' But now you see them, they work for low wages, in abominable conditions—no toilets, makeshift sheds with the sun in their faces, thatched roofs in the rain. Some travel an hour by bus and the rest of the way by foot to reach the sites. They persevere, they adapt and create. These women are the strength of Mobile Creches."

As for Indu herself, she is engaged in a perpetual guerilla action. Construction magnates, site engineers, municipal authorities can look out the window of their palatial offices or their polished Mercedes without seeing that a large number of laborers slogging through the mud are women—and that therefore the law requires provision of a creche. "Madame," they say, "please send me all the correspondence, I will be writing to you." One element that keeps Indu going is surely her wicked sense of humor.

"I live in one of those residential towers," she says. "You know the kind. The residents can take their dogs in the elevator, but not their servants. When we moved into the first building, some of the others were still under construction. A creche was operating there, that we had established after eight months' negotiations. Whenever I appeared, I was followed by swarms of children. The new residents kept me at arms' length. 'What are you, an *ayah?*' they asked." Indu laughs with glee. "My neighbors don't understand me *at all.*"

◆ ◆ ◆

Can a sensitive, civic-minded woman make a social commitment without becoming either a maverick or a saint? Many unheroic young women graduating from universities do not wish simply to stay at home and raise bright children. And they object to the assumptions of traditional voluntary organizations for "social uplift." A few find places in institutes or associations engaged in some aspect of women's development. SEWA, for example, requires educated English-speaking women for fund raising, proposal writing, publishing, legal aid, accountancy, and the like. One such staff member told me, "We feel strongly about the way women are placed, how they are treated. We need to do something constructive about it, even if we have no economic need to work. In a way, we are rebelling too against the expectations placed on us."

Working in an organization for women's development may eventually mean interacting with rural women, who are, after all, the vast majority. This is a venture into a foreign territory, so great are the differences in experience and expectations between educated urban and illiterate rural women. Field workers from one action-oriented research institute, who had gone out freshly versed in methodology and full of ideals, had a rude time of it. They met dogged resistance, overt manipulation, utter indifference. Their respondents, hoping for reward, duly spouted whatever they thought the researchers wanted to hear. But a stint of living in the isolation and penury of the village made them more understanding, especially when they caught themselves behaving in similar ways. "You have to live that life to understand how a villager will want to grab anything that's offered that comes from outside. You yourself become so needy—let someone bring me a newspaper, any little thing from the outside world."

To be in the company of vigorous and committed women is a heady experience. One begins to be persuaded that a grand awakening is at hand, green shoots emerging in unlikely places; women at every level are standing taller, recovering their powers, reaching out to each other across crumbling barriers of caste and class.

This depends on what lens you are looking through. A feminist columnist cites a "tremendous mental change" among the many readers who write to her and reports, on returning from a lecture tour, that the Muslim women are seething under their burkahs. "Strikingly vibrant working-class feminism [is] spreading through the western and southern parts of the country," writes a Marxist intellectual. "One feels a current of exhilaration running through the accounts of researchers and activists involved with the multitude of struggles and innovative mobilization processes."[3]

There is a palpable exhilaration, and it is energizing. But many women embroiled in the struggle are too weary to fire off dispatches. They know how scattered the gains are, how profound the passivity, and how many-armed the resistance. No cost-effectiveness criteria—cost of effort for result obtained—can be applied to gauge the utility and necessity of working for the women's cause in India.

In every generation, certain daughters of socially prominent or orthodox Brahman families repudiate the life decreed for them and go to live in parched villages and organize cooperatives or develop artisanal industry in remote tribal districts. Once, these were isolated cases, like the legendary ascetics, performing austerities to re-equilibrate the order of things. Today, they too can be seen as part of a vast informal network, a movement, whose discords and differences of approach are symptomatic of its vitality.

All this will no doubt look scraggly and sound shrill from the vantage point of Tara's gorgeous living room. Thick drapes of pale silk brocade can be drawn to block the view. But movement there is: its victories are modest but definitive; its motto, in the words of one activist, "to keep on keeping on." And it is sufficiently visible and numerous for at least two ambitious "reformist" politicians to have begun paying it court.[4] Perhaps these men have perceived the link between traditional notions of woman power—the ready reference to shakti, to goddess—and contemporary activism: women's effective power.

• 15 •

A FOUR-THOUSAND-YEAR-OLD HISTORY

Strengthened by my thoughts of you,
travel an unthreatened path: for if a thing
must be, good women are not timorous.

—Kunti to Draupadi, Mahabharata

We are sitting in the pitch dark, on the lawn of a modest bungalow near Delhi University. There is a power blackout, as there has been every day, sector by sector, throughout the city. Some say that New Delhi is voluntarily cutting its consumption to divert electric power to the irrigation pumps in the vast parched farmbelt to the north. Others maintain that political bosses in the drought-afflicted states have blocked the flow from the hydroelectric plants further north to embarrass the government and put pressure on a capital whose nights are already tense with terrorist shooting sprees.

The three of us are tranquil in the darkness, refreshed by the cooling night air after a hectic day. Though we meet rarely, our friendship goes back to the 1960s in Cambridge, Massachusetts. Deben is a Bengali intellectual of the old school, indifferent to worldly goods (other than books), a demanding thinker but amiable in company, never doctrinaire. His wife Rupa is rooted in the same tradition and possessed of similar integrity and restraint. For thirty years, she has taught and done research, but her primary vocation has been helpmate and companion. Rupa is a very private person who keeps her own counsel but sometimes gives glimpses of banked fires.

She and I had met in town that day for lunch. Between the soup and the toasted sandwiches, a ninety-minute power cut had intervened. We barely noticed it, so much did we have to catch up on and say to each other. Then, Rupa wanted to go buy an Orissi sari for her daughter, who is studying abroad. I planned to attend an anti-sati seminar at the Legal Institute. We did both, careening from place to place in scooter rickshaws. Evening found us trekking a kilometer to find a taxi, under a sky blurred to sepia as the fumes of rush hour corroded the sunset.

In the taxi, Rupa recounted a discovery she had made while analyzing Indian demographic data. Despite a marked decrease in infant mortality and a considerable advance in overall life expectancy, the ratio of females to males was low and even declining. Female mortality was highest in the fifteen to forty-five age range, the marriage and child-bearing years. This trend was particularly marked in the four states of the "Hindu heartland" that Rupa referred to as "the bastion of north Indian patriarchy."

The fact that, unknown to her, studies of this phenomenon had already been published, did not matter. Like me, Rupa was making her own discoveries. Recently, she said, she had been turning away from statistical analysis to a more field-oriented approach. She had sent her students, armed with questionnaires, to interview the women who labored the farmland at the city limits. The first thing the students found was how inappropriate—incomprehensible—were some of their questions; for example, "What do you do in your leisure time?"

All this gnawed at Rupa. It seemed not only to call for a larger conceptual framework but also to involve implications for her own life as a woman. There was much to explore, but we were late arriving at the house, and Deben, who held a highly responsible administrative post, had left his office early to see me.

Over tea, in the kitchen by candlelight, the talk was more

general. We exchanged news of children, gossiped about friends, and surveyed the international scene. But back on the dark lawn, our disembodied voices took up the day's themes. We spoke of social calamity and political incompetence, of the tragic waste of human potential in India, and the urgent need for structural change that would liberate and engage the energies of women. "Ah, yes," said Deben, reclining in his canvas chair. "But you forget: we have a four-thousand-year-old history."

Like a great sculpted weight, the Hindu heritage descended—as justification, as authority, as rationale for acceptance or despair. Men formed at the best universities in India, Britain, the United States—scientists, business executives, a psychiatrist—had told me, each with an avuncular smile: "Things can't be hurried here." "Mentalities are not going to change." "We have a four-thousand-year-old history."

Is it not this megalith that women are scraping and chipping away at, with heroic persistence and improvised tools?

Item: An urban women's cooperative had been trying for months to obtain petty loans on a group guarantee basis from an authorized bank, but the bank officers just never found time to meet their representatives. This same bank was promoting a small savings scheme, inviting low-income persons to open accounts with a minimum deposit of five rupees each. One morning, the bank clerks unlocked their windows to find long lines of women waiting. Each had come to open a savings account, and each had five rupees in the form of one hundred five-paise coins—nearly weightless metal flakes that had to be counted and stacked before the papers could be drawn up. Standing with patient dignity, their knotted handkerchiefs full of paise, the 150 women had the tellers immobilized. No other business could be transacted.

After one hour, the bank manager came out with his hands up, figuratively speaking. He had the leaders of the women's group called to his office, and the loan formalities were initiated.

A contrasting item: Two hundred million rupees were handed out to fifty thousand beneficiaries, largely tribal and scheduled-caste women, in a rural district in the course of a loan *mela*. A mela is a fair or festival, most often a collective religious rite, with all its colorful trappings. A loan mela is a modern variant that draws huge crowds—some for handouts, many just for the excitement. During the mela, commercial and cooperative banks of the area, heavily subsidized by the government, dispense small loans to deserving applicants. In this case, district and bank officials had canvassed in two thousand villages, talking up the prospect of three- or four-thousand rupee loans. Whether the individuals, largely illiterate and dirt poor, had a proposal, a means of carrying it through, or a clear idea that loan means repayment with interest, did not matter. The operation was primarily political, engineered by the Congress (I) member of parliament from the area. All the appurtenances of the mela—posters, banners, vehicles—displayed the symbol and colors of the then ruling party.

For a short time after, life is easier for the citizens of the district, and they know whom they have to thank. But the long-term results are all too predictable. Individual recipients setting out ad hoc to breed goats or produce petty commodities are likely to run into problems. Repayments will dwindle; the default rate will be high. In the resulting muddle and waste, male officialdom will have its opinion of illiterate low-caste women amply confirmed.

A loan mela is an extravaganza of dubious efficacy but with a powerful hold on the popular imagination. What canny women have been able to perform is unspectacular, by comparison. Yet it is quietly spectacular.

A venerable scholar, an authority on the Vedas, was holding court beside a Shiva temple in 1988. He confirmed that women and Harijans are banned from studying Vedic texts. He extolled sati, proclaiming that a wife who voluntarily immolates herself earns precisely thirty-five billion years of happiness and salvation for her husband's and father's families. The sage had agreed to have a press conference. But when women reporters stood up to challenge him, he fixed their wagon: he would answer only those persons who could repeat verbatim, in Sanskrit, his reply to the previous question.

"He made our blood boil," said one journalist.

Like so many Indian situations, the encounter between old sage and young scribe had its comic and its appalling aspects.

Still, no woman had ever publicly crossed swords with him. Newspaper reports were more than sympathetic: they labeled the Hindu priest obscurantist, misogynist, and even called for his arrest.

A news item from Punjab follows (some names deleted).

> Nine-year-old Kuljit Kaur of T. village was recently married to Bagha (25), the polio-stricken son of W. S. of N. village. This marriage, in violation of the Child Marriage Restriction Act, was brought to the notice of the authorities.
>
> The widowed mother of the girl, Maya, an Assamese, and Pratap Singh, a brother of the girl, had arranged the marriage. The news of the marriage had reached Surjeet Kaur, an aunt of the girl, as Pratap Singh had gone to her village to hire a photographer.
>
> Surjeet Kaur and her husband lodged a protest with the sarpanch [head man] of T. village. The panchayat [village assembly] declared the marriage illegal. It was learnt that Rs. 2,000 had been paid to the girl's mother who refused to hand over the girl to her uncle and aunt.
>
> The matter was brought to the notice of the Punjab Istri Sabha who sought police help. Arrested were Maya, Bagha, Pratap Singh, and Bagha's father and the go-betweens. The minor girl was handed over to her aunt.
>
> The granthi [priest] who performed the marriage was not arrested. The mother, however, pleaded guilty. It is learnt that she was leading an unhappy life and had planned to return to Assam with the money. The local Istri Sabha and the trade union would help rehabilitate the family.

Is this the story of how a backward mother sold off her female child for monetary gain?

Or is this the story: A mother with no resources, living far from her homeland, is reduced to the status of nonperson by the death of her husband. Seeing little hope of social insertion or even survival for her daughter, she tries to assure the child's future in the only way she knows, by providing her with a husband. The sister of the child's father alerts the elected village authority, which acts promptly to apply the law. Arrests are made—not, significantly, of the priest, but of all the secular players. Functioning in the village structure are organisms that can provide assistance and follow-up: a trade union, and, interestingly, a women's council (Istri Sabha). The story's headline, "9-year-old girl married off" plays up the sensational aspect. But in fact this tale tells of progress and of the extent to which mentalities can and do change.

The daily press often carries stories, dealing with women and evidently deemed newsworthy, that depict clashes of values and assumptions, often with dramatic consequences. Far more numerous are the everyday, unrecorded dramas of confrontation between "modernity" and "tradition."

Rupa told me about the eldest daughter of an orthodox Jain family of her acquaintance. Two words sum up the young woman's existential predicament: she was dark and bright. Her parents could not find a well-educated suitor of acceptable caste who would marry a girl who was not fair-skinned. The girl said, "Find me anyone. I don't wish to stand in the way of family happiness or prejudice the marriages of my younger sisters."

Eventually, she was wed to an engineer who had a history of mental illness. After the marriage, the in-laws permitted the bride to return to the university to finish her master's degree. In her absence, the young man swallowed a bottle of sleeping pills and died. His family did not lay the blame for his suicide on the young woman's bad karma. Nor did her parents, in taking her back, insist that she observe the white-shrouded isolation of the husband-deprived. But in the eyes of the community, her fate was sealed. What man would have her now—widowed, dark, and bright?

Rupa, with her faultless intellectual and brahmanic credentials, was able to lead the daughter and the mother to look critically at the traditions of their caste. They no longer find it unthinkable that the young woman could live independently or marry again. But for the larger community in which she must live, she is considered fortunate to be able to stay with her parents and earn her keep as an unassuming school teacher for the rest of her days. She will eventually have the consolation of nephews and nieces and perhaps the companionship of other widows and spinsters. She may seek emotional release in elaborate religiosity or attachment to a guru. Blocked in her performance of the culturally defined womanly role, she is likely to have an image of herself as a burden, a failure, an inauspicious one. As V. S. Naipaul observed in *A*

House for Mr. Biswas (160), for such women, "ambition, if the word could be used, was a series of negatives: not to be unmarried, not to be childless, not to be an undutiful daughter, sister, wife, mother, widow." Thus has the culture instructed her, for the better part of these four thousand years.

And this is construed in a positive light. The dynamic women of this century who have spoken out for female education, abolition of caste, national independence, and equal rights for women, have, with few exceptions, been arch-defenders of traditional domesticity. Within the home, they are deferential and discreet, respecting the reigning hierarchy of males and elders. Serenely certain of their roles and proud of their competencies, such women know their value. They look with condescension, even pity, at Western women, struggling in the snares of an illusory "liberation."

Today, there are militant feminists, refusers and reformers, who see the fortress-family in a different light. But they are not about to attack it head on. To introduce a challenge from a seemingly detached, Western-educated point of view would be not only bad strategy but also a profound misreading of the tradition itself. As Madhu Kishwar writes in *In Search of Answers* (46) the effort must be made "to begin to separate the devastating aspects from the points of strength within cultural traditions, and start using the strengths to transform the traditions." The preconditions for struggle, in Niloufer Bhagwat's terms, are created by projecting not the morbidity, but the strength of Indian women to deal with their oppression. The strengths are many, and some of the most effective strategies for eliciting them involve exploiting the historic and legendary pasts.

There is no lack of historical models among the pioneering social reformers of the nineteenth and early twentieth centuries. These women crusaded against female illiteracy and child marriage, founded welfare societies, edited magazines for women, and spoke out against religious dogmatism. They are honored as the "first wave." Their contemporary appeal is somewhat limited by the fact that they were protected upper-caste women, ultimately dependent on the forward-looking husbands and/or fathers who encouraged them. But their lives and works are instructive and important, and their legacy very much alive.

More present to the popular imagination are the heroic *ranis*, Rajput and Maratha princesses who ruled over clans, administered cities, and led armies into battle. The Maharani of Indore, who reigned from 1765 to 1795, and the swashbuckling Rani of Jhansi, who died in combat against the British foe in 1858, are among the most celebrated. Recent years have seen an upsurge of interest in these real-life heroines. Feminist historians portray them as *virangana*, the woman who manifests qualities of *virya* (heroism)—bravery and virtue—and whose status is not defined by relation to a man. [1]

The viranganas of fact and folklore are not all lofty ladies. They include rebels on horseback and bandit queens. A staple item of Hindi films of the 1930s, "tough-guy" women made a comeback in the late 1980s. Top box-office stars, once bejewelled and kittenish, appeared in black leather, packing pistols, and spoiling for revenge. They were out to punish rapists, and they'd shoot below the belt. Ironically dubbed "women-oriented," these formula films, made by men, titillated a largely male audience. The macho heroine had a chance to turn the tables and demonstrate that male/female relations are a simple matter of force—dominate or be dominated. The male viewer, after three hours of wide-screen mayhem committed by a slinky avengeress, might be moved to go straight home and batter his wife.

But the star who played the greatest number of roles as outlaw or killer cop declared herself satisfied. "Times have changed, thank God," she was quoted in *India Today* (July 15, 1988). "For the first time the heroine has emerged as a strong, tough woman willing to fight back, reflecting the Indian woman of today."

A more credible approach to constructing an empowering history for Indian women is in the reinterpretation of sanctified female figures of the mythohistorical past. These include the learned women of the Upanishads and the paragons of the epics, particularly Sita and Draupadi. In a feminist perspective, their virtues can be appreciated anew: they are fair-minded, courageous, intelligent, and independent of spirit. To model oneself on one of these great figures means refusing to bend to arbitrary male authority and heeding the voice of one's own conscience.

This is not the first time that the epic heroines have been

recruited as symbols in the cause of liberation. During the "Quit India" movement and the struggle for national self-determination, Gandhi cited the "robust independence" of Draupadi and Sita's capacities for nonviolent resistance. He called upon women to emulate these archetypes and display the superior moral and physical courage that he knew they had. Women like Sarojini Naidu, one of Gandhi's lieutenants, amply confirmed his faith and became national heroines in their own right.

The profound ambiguities in Gandhi's attitude toward women have been recognized and discussed.[2] On the one hand, as Madhu Kishwar notes, "He tried changing women's position without transforming their relation to the outer world of production or the inner world of family, sexuality and reproduction." On the other hand, Gandhi is generally credited with giving the women's cause moral legitimacy, easing the entry of women into public life, and actively helping create the conditions for liberation from domestic bondage.

Now, over forty years after his death, pious lip service continues. But Gandhi's living legacy is in women's cooperatives, service-oriented ashrams, and grassroots action/research organizations that practice Gandhian principles. Their leaders have achieved visibility and a modest amount of clout, especially now that women's roles are perceived as crucial in Third World development and defense of natural resources. When Ela Bhatt of SEWA is appointed to a government commission or speaks to an international assembly, her name is in the papers. In India, exemplary individuals can exert a strong influence.

Today's women's movement can thus cite its historical antecedents and powerful cultural referents and legitimately claim Gandhi's blessing. It is a movement whose time had come; within six years after the creation of the first women's studies units (1980), there had blossomed over a hundred research organizations, action groups, and resource centers dedicated to "women's issues."[3] Today's militants are well aware of one drawback: historically, the impetus for change has come from a privileged urban class, more secular and Western-oriented than the rest and with only superficial knowledge of the lives of the rural masses. Efforts are being made to breach the barrier. Urban resource centers establish antennae in surrounding villages. Conventions are held in backward states or provincial capitals rather than in the vanguard cities. Rural women's cooperatives are being initiated on a wide scale. Research done on the laboring proletariat is conceived not as an end in itself, but as a springboard for intervention and identification of grass-roots leaders. Such leaders as they emerge may have very different agendas from the urban academics and feminists. But this reflects the larger Indian reality: the ever-present gap between the "eternal" village and city India, galvanized by modernization. The chronic imbalance is reinforced by today's turbulent economic development; moreover, opportunity tends to favor the advantaged. Where women are concerned, the likely changes are those transitions that do not really challenge structures or certitudes.

Amrita, eldest daughter of a wealthy Punjabi, has a flair for business and wants to make a career. Her father is delighted to support the cost of her master's degree. Amrita will carry on the family tradition and enhance her value on the marriage market at the same time. It is a question not of self-realization, but of maximizing resources. Should she at some point find herself on her own, Amrita will never become a financial burden. She is safely settled, come what may.

But what about Sudha, whose father is night-watchman in Amrita's apartment building? Sudha was the first girl in her slum to complete tenth grade. At eighteen, she put herself on the job market and passed the test for telephone operator. She is cocky about her prospects: after all, no other female in her shantytown can speak English. Sudha does not know that of nine thousand other candidates for the job many have the advantage of coming from the lower middle class. She is now too highly qualified to marry a manual laborer or a farmer in her natal village. Yet she has no access to introductions elsewhere. All eyes are now upon her and her ambitious parents. If Sudha does not land a white-collar job or a white-collar husband, then everyone will know just what good it does to educate daughters.

Amrita will soon join her peers in the Association of Women Entrepreneurs and in the city Chamber of Commerce.

Sudha is in danger of falling into no-woman's land. It is a risk run by the woman whose intellectual attainment is incommensurate with her social standing, who allows her education to influence the way she thinks and behaves. Such women may know what shackles they wish to break without realizing what safety ropes may be severed. Many a middle-class homemaker will do her best to guard against such a situation developing under her roof.

Companionate mom of two planned children, the modern urban mother has emancipated herself from tedious ritual observances and has streamlined her domestic routines. But the accommodations she has made to changing social realities do not necessarily indicate a progressive attitude. She may consciously cling to conservative standards, especially in rearing her daughters. Separateness and status are safe bulwarks in a world of debased values, odd social amalgams, and junk culture. Not only outside pressure but also inner conviction may hold her to her age-old role of tradition bearer, guardian of the dharma.

The Indian sociologist André Béteille distinguishes between *modernistic* and *modernizing*. "To the extent that an elite has acquired merely the symbols and styles of life, or even the skills of high status groups in more advanced societies, it is *modernistic*. It becomes *modernizing* only when it succeeds in utilizing these skills in a socially significant way."[4]

Truly modernizing women like Indu Balagopal, Madhu Kishwar, Niloufer Bhagwat, and Prema Purao are liberated. They have no fear of social sanction. They have solid credentials in the social hierarchy, are well educated, and have been encouraged by fathers, husbands, or mentors. They are equipped to march out and stake claims to new territories, to transgress the norms. From the very bottom of the social pyramid comes an echo of this force and this audacity. Women in utter poverty, with no social position to defend, can gain much as activists. They have nothing to lose. Mothers, breadwinners, citizens, once engaged they also throw themselves into the struggle without a backward glance.

The great mass of women do not enjoy this opportunity or immunity. They sense the irrepressible ferment and quest; and just as surely they are dissuaded by the specter of no-woman's land. To navigate between the two, in one's daily life, can be dangerous.

Mamta, a bright young woman with limited education, found her way to a women's resource center. She soon became a dedicated liaison worker between the center and the mill workers' tenement where she lived. Mamta had one daughter and a good husband to whom she dreamed of giving a son. But after two miscarriages and a tubal pregnancy, she had been strongly advised not to risk another.

Her feminist friends showed her scientific diagrams of her insides and recommended that she be sterilized. Her tenement friends were equally convincing. They knew that Mamta's ill fortune came from the fact that she paid no homage to the local goddess, whose icon was particularly auspicious. At least two women had obtained sons by devoted worship. Arrogant Mamta, blessed with good health and a loving husband, was being punished for her impiety.

Mamta thought it over and settled on a compromise. She gave equal time to each, the women's center and the goddess, left off birth control, and ended up in emergency surgery for ablation of the uterus. From both camps her friends came to the hospital to donate blood.

Brave departures can have bitter aftermaths. And many women see no alternative to four-thousand-year-old imperatives of duty and honor, of family name, of economic necessity—backed by either the threat or the fact of violence. Yet it is striking how many women one meets have a true story to tell of a protest or initiative of someone from their own workplace or neighborhood. Quite spontaneously, a woman tells the story. Then, emboldened by the telling, she may add, shy or proud, or just to indicate the leanings of her own heart:

"You see, I am like this, but I'm not letting it happen to my younger sister."

Or, "I have raised my daughters differently. They won't end up like me."

Coda

AGAINST a background of global depredation perceived by feminists and others as the consequence of male sovereignty—and specifically, white occidental male sovereignty—over the earth, a mythic figure is emerging. She is the Third World Woman. An idealized composite, she is physically sound, morally valiant, in tune with nature, sustaining and safeguarding the web of life. In her everlasting struggle to keep clean, fit for work, and able to nurture children, she is awakening to the force that dwells within her: not merely the strength to endure, but an elemental female power. In its potential to transform and transcend, this power, this shakti, is assimilated with the goddess.

"If the world is to find a way out," says a noted Indian feminist, "an actor must be identified whose self-empowerment will of itself give birth to new alternatives and new methods in development. This actor—and to many she will seem perhaps the most unlikely of all—is the poor Third World woman."[1] Bringing about profound social change through new networks of female solidarity, drawing spiritual sustenance from her identification with the goddess, this collective heroine has the potential to accomplish on the global scale what she has humbly been doing on the family and village level: nurture, energize, and redeem.

Since ancient times, this feminine capability has been disparaged, diverted, occulted. Men have not only monopolized the control of the political economy, but they have also appropriated the goddess-fabrik. Priests and politicians, colonial governors and native patriots—phallocrats all—have manipulated the traditional representations of the mother goddess, harnessing her powers to their own ends. For this reason, goddess worship and the goddess cults that have flourished throughout history have had no enhancing effect on the status or options of ordinary women. The Great Tradition has been established, codified, and transmitted, from father to son. But as women begin to repossess the goddess, they will both revalorize themselves and generate the ethical structures that could spell survival for the global family and the planet.

This vision has some familiar elements: nostalgia for a simpler age of peace and harmony; consecration of a chosen people, humble of heart, ennobled by suffering, and closest to the Deity. The temptation of the visionary is understandably strong. It carries a healing and replenishing message to women everywhere. Its source is in our profound exasperation; it is balm for deep wounds.

But is it the basis of a program?

The apotheosized Third World woman is the creation of relatively privileged feminists of many nations, women who recognize a need to reach out and claim links with the most despised and oppressed of the gender. This vision attributes to subsistence-level women a talent for nurture, a special sensitivity to the rhythms of nature and to all living things. It assumes that by now patriarchal systems are generally recognized to be ponderous dinosaurs and women are the life-enhancers, the virtuosae. Invested with the power as well as the responsibility, they seem to incorporate a new version of shakti and streedharma. In the full sway of her sexual and spiritual powers, woman regenerates and lights the way for humankind.

She seems to be alone. Have men proved so tiresomely demanding and narcissistic, so ineffectual and obstructive, that they are best left to go play with their toys (rendered nonlethal) so that the women can get on with it? Is there not a danger here of falling into men's old trick of exclusivity, relegating the Other to a position of inferiority and insignificance, and thus assuring the alienation of men?

It is indeed high time that women recuperate the goddess and retrieve the confidence and self-esteem to liberate themselves, Third World women and all women, from the patriarchal yoke. But it is foolhardy to assume that the empowered woman will be nurturing and benign, never willful, abusive, or self-intoxicated—as is, sometimes, the goddess herself. The "way out" that has been suggested can be only very partial unless it also aspires to the equity and mutuality in gender relations that so far have eluded all our scenarios.

✦ ✦ ✦

In the empty lot behind the apartment buildings, my neighbors are playing Holi. Holi, the festival that ushers in the spring, is a day of provocations and reversals. Hierarchy goes topsy-turvy: servants insult their masters, students command their teachers, wives defy husbands, in a ritual exchange of roles. In city neighborhoods, there are no rustic practical jokes, like sluicing elders with pails of diluted dung. Instead, there is a free-for-all dousing with bright powders and colored water.

Soon after sunrise, the children were already outside with full paper cones, spraying one another with red, green, and blue powder. By noon, every man, woman, and child had rainbow hair and streaked, clownlike faces. Now, after a pause for lunch and clean-up, community sports and games are taking place on the splotched and trampled grass. The mothers, who have put on clean saris after the morning's exuberance, organize children's relay races. From the sidelines, they cheer on the duck-walkers, the peanut-pushers; they laugh at the ill-assorted pairs of girls, with one long leg and one short leg bound by a red scarf, who lurch toward the finish line.

After the children's races comes the ladies' event: musical chairs. Some men begin to open folding chairs in a grand circle; others round up the ladies. A few women demur, or try to demur, reluctant to make a spectacle of themselves. But this is Holi, the day when throwing off constraints is one's right and duty. Smiling or solemn-faced, about twenty women are corralled into a circle. The men call the tune, with harmonica, bamboo flute, and drum. The pace is dignified at first. There is just a flurry at the instant when the music halts. One woman out, one chair withdrawn. A slightly faster cadence, and the women navigating among the chairs turn in a reduced space with their sandals slapping the ground. The music stops short and takes them by surprise. A woman lunges, nearly tipping the chair she lands in—and someone is eliminated. Six, five, four—they are concentrating now, out of breath and excited. The music resumes. Little children wander through the circle and get in the way. But, of course, children are never in the way.

Now there are only two women left, and a single chair. A crowd has gathered. "Good show, Renuka!" "Go it, Nalini!" Nalini, large and rumpled, is panting for breath. Renuka blots the sweat on her nose and upper lip and tucks her damp hanky back into the waist of her sari, where it is also damp. They are told to get on their marks for the last round.

For a moment, each one feels giddy, invaded by the glad, light feeling that belongs to the time she was a schoolgirl on the playing field, in white socks and gym bloomers, giving her all for team and for school. Once again, she is that lean, long-legged girl, free of impedimenta—unappropriated and inviolate.

Then the men take up the tune, and the women scurry.

Notes

1. THE DANCE OF MAYURI

1. See especially Rama Mehta, *The Western-Educated Indian Woman.*

6. INGREDIENTS OF EVERYDAY LIFE

1. In a study by Neera Desai, reported in Maria Mies, *Indian Women and Patriarchy,* 182.
2. See Girija Khanna and Mariamma A. Verghese, *Indian Women Today,* 64.
3. Shakti Editorial Collective, *In Search of Our Bodies,* 101.
4. Quoted by Khanna and Verghese, *Indian Women Today,* 49.
5. R. K. Nayyar, producer, and Sudha Chandran, actress, quoted in *India Today,* August 15, 1988, 108. There is an ironic footnote to this. Sudha Chandran ("Rekha") is the actress/dancer whose earlier fictionalized autobiographical film *Mayuri* (see pp. 8–10) conveyed a very different message.

7. FEMALE PROWESS: SHAKTI

1. Extracts from the "Hymn to Creation," *Rig-Veda* X, 129. Trans. Arthur L. Basham, *The Wonder That Was India,* 247–248.
2. Heinrich Zimmer, *Myths and Symbols in Indian Art and Civilization,* 25.
3. The reader is referred to the works of Wendy Doniger O'Flaherty, especially *Asceticism and Eroticism in the Mythology of Shiva* (London: Oxford University Press, 1973) and *Women, Androgynes and Other Mythical Beasts* (Chicago: University of Chicago Press, 1980).
4. Interpretations of Heinrich Zimmer and Ananda Coomaraswamy, cited by Vassilis G. Vitsaxis, *Hindu Epics, Myths and Legends in Popular Illustration,* 91.
5. Zimmer, *Myths and Symbols,* 96. The distinguished Sanskrit scholar Heinrich Zimmer died in 1943. One can only remain intrigued by this last remark and by the sensitivity of much of his interpretation.
6. Veena Das, "The Goddess and the Demon, an analysis of the Devi Mahatmya," *Manushi* 30(1985): 28–32.

8. FEMALE PROPRIETY: STREEDHARMA

1. A. L. Basham, *The Wonder That Was India,* 407.
2. C. Rajagopalachari, trans., *Ramayana,* 174.
3. Sudhir Kakar, *The Inner World,* 63–64.
4. Sita means *furrow,* a universal symbol for the vagina. While my aim here is to indicate how myths can influence identity formation and behavior, a

more thoroughgoing psychoanalytic reading of the tale yields rich insights. For this, the reader is referred to Sudhir Kakar, *The Inner World*, to whom I am indebted for some observations in this chapter.

5. "Here is my daughter, Sita, who will ever tread with you the path of *dharma*. Take her hand in yours. Blessed and devoted, she will ever walk with you like your own shadow." Rajagopalachari, *Ramayana*, 44.

6. H. P. Shastri, trans., *Ramayana*, 1, 233. Quoted in Sudhir Kakar, *The Inner World*, 65.

7. Lanka is today Sri Lanka, and in ancient days, the home of dark-skinned, meat-eating aborigines whose savage ways were anathema to light-skinned, martially disciplined Aryans.

8. Rajagopalachari, *Ramayana*, 166.

9. Quoted by Vassilis G. Vitsaxis, *Hindu Epics*, 36.

10. Ibid.

11. Kakar, *The Inner World*, 218, n. 30.

12. Ibid., 63.

13. Ibid., 217, n. 9.

14. *Mahabharata*, 5, 30, 6.

15. *Mahabharata* (Bombay ed.) 1, 74, 40ff. Both verses trans., A. L. Basham, *The Wonder That Was India*, 182.

16. *The Laws of Manu*, trans. G. Buhler, in Kakar, *The Inner World*, 93.

17. Quoted in Kakar, *The Inner World*, 76.

18. *The Laws of Manu*, quoted in Richard Lannoy, *The Speaking Tree*, 103.

19. *Ramayana*, 7, 97, quoted in David Kinsley, *Hindu Goddesses*, 76.

9. THE EPIC WIFE

1. *Mahabharata*, trans. P. C. Roy, 1, 193, 381.

2. *Mahabharata*, trans. R. K. Narayan, 41.

3. Readers acquainted with the translations of the *Mahabharata* based on texts of existing Northern manuscripts will find only an abbreviated reference to this tale. The full version, in 118 lines, appears in the "Southern recension," the collation of all existing manuscripts written in the languages of South India. The scholarly controversy about the authenticity of the two compilations is reviewed in the preface of the definitive (Poona) edition of the *Mahabharata*. Here, the editor points out that in general, the Southern texts are richer in information, "fuller, more exuberant, more ornate," while the Northern version tends to be more lofty and vague—perhaps with the intention of being more elevating.

From the psychological and dramatic points of view, the story of Nalayani/Draupadi is too suggestive to leave aside, and this is no doubt why R. K. Narayan features it prominently in his condensed prose version of the Epic. I follow Narayan's text here (41ff.), which is based on the P. P. S. Sastri edition of the *Mahabharata*. For all the noncontroversial episodes where differences are only in the wording of the English translations, the source is the P. C. Roy translation.

4. Draupadi explains that she picked up all this knowledge by monitoring her brothers' discussions of what they had learned from their Brahman teachers, by absorbing the words of the pundits who came to visit her father, upon whose lap she sat, and by posing questions herself whenever she was sent on errands to a scholar's home. Thus, the sharp-witted little girl was able to educate herself.
5. This and the following texts are from the P. C. Roy translation, 3, 231, 472–474.

10. POWER AND CONTAINMENT

1. *The Lay of the Anklet (Silappadigaram)*, trans. V. R. R. Dikshitar. Lines quoted are from Basham, *The Wonder That Was India*, 470–474.
2. *Virtue* in the wider signification of the French *vertu:* (a) strength, force of character; (b) inner disposition to do good and avoid doing evil; (c) modesty, chastity.
3. Tara Ali Baigh, *India's Woman Power*, 131–135 (italics added).
4. Frieda Hauswirth (Das), *Purdah, the Status of Indian Women*, 108.
5. Khanna and Verghese, *Indian Women Today*, 33–34.
6. *The Ten Princes (Dasakumaracita)*, 11, trans. A. Ryder, and quoted in Basham, *The Wonder That Was India*, 446.
7. Kakar, *The Inner World*, is enlightening in this regard; see especially its chapters 3 and 4 and Appendix.
8. A telling example of this is given by Jocelyn Kynch and Amartya Sen, in "Indian women, well-being and survival." A year after the Bengal famine of 1943, a health survey team conducting medical examinations asked people to describe their own state of health. Many widows and widowers were in the sample. When asked to specify, nearly half the widowers claimed to be either "ill" or "in indifferent health," while only 2.5 percent of the widows said this was their case. When those claiming to be ill were left aside and the others requestioned, 45 percent of the men described their state of health as "indifferent"—and not one of the women!

The famine had not played favorites. Being in a depleted and fatigued state was perceived as normal by the widows. Had they been asked to assess the health of the men, one suspects that they would have commiserated and found the poor chaps to be quite below par!

11. ONLY A FEMALE

1. Quoted in Madhu Kishwar and Ruth Vanita, *In Search of Answers*, 203.
2. See Malini Karkal, "How the other half dies in Bombay," *Economic and Political Weekly*, 20, no. 34 (August 24, 1985): 1424.
3. See *India Today*, February 29, 1988, 38. This event, along with grisly photos, was widely covered and deplored in the Indian press.
4. *Atharvaveda*, 3, 23, 2–4.
5. Margaret Cormack, *The Hindu Woman*, 41.
6. A law strictly curbing prenatal sex determination tests was passed in

1988 in the state of Maharashtra, whose capital is Bombay. Although the law has its loopholes, and enforcement is always a question, the existence of any law at all is due to pressure brought by feminist and other women's groups.

7. Bachi J. Karkaria, "Only a Girl," *Statesman Miscellany* (Calcutta), November 17, 1985, 3–4.

8. Shanti Ghosh, "Born to Die," *Statesman Miscellany*, November 24, 1985.

9. Ibid.

10. Work being done in pluridisciplinary fields like women's studies and development studies questions traditional assumptions and methodologies and proposes new research domains. See, for example, Jocelyn Kynch and Amartya Sen, "Indian Women," with its bibliography, and Devaki Jain and Nirmala Banerjee, *Tyranny of the Household*.

11. Photographs published in *Manushi* and elsewhere catch the accused husband with either a smirk on his face or an obtuse expression that seems to ask what all the fuss is about. In a precedent-setting judgment in 1989, the Supreme Court widened the interpretation of "abetment to suicide" in domestic maltreatment cases. See Geeta Luthra and Pinky Anand, "Torture is Abetment of Suicide," *Manushi* 54–55 (September–December 1989): 22–24.

12. Manini Das, "Women against Dowry," in Kishwar and Vanita, *In Search of Answers*, 225–226.

13. Mrs. P. K., a "daughter-in-law baiter," is quoted in 1989: "Girls have to take it. They are made for sacrifice. All this *naye zenane ki bat* [new women's talk] that girls are equal to boys is alright in books but . . . any girl who believes in it is stupid. Men are made by nature to get obedience from their wives. . . . That is what our *shastras* teach." S. Lalitha, "Bride and Prejudice," *The Times of India*, lifestyle section, September 16, 1989.

14. Richard Lannoy, *The Speaking Tree*, 130.

12. TO CHANGE YOUR OWN LIFE

1. The existence of child abuse has also been ignored or denied. In a feature article on the subject in *India Today* (January 31, 1987), together with explicit photos and case histories is the statement of a leading doctor in a major city: "Child abuse does not take place in India. I have not seen a single case in the last thirty years" (69).

13. THE COLLECTIVE VENTURE

1. *Manushi* 32 (January–February 1986): 34–40.

2. Quoted in *Self-Employed Women's Association* (pamphlet), published by SEWA, Ahmedabad, 1984, 13–14.

3. Ibid., 15–16.

4. Maitreyi Krishna Raj, "Approaches to self-reliance for women," 41.

5. The Working Women's Forum, Madras, is another case in point. Rural and urban women's collectives are coming up all over the country. The two described here are particularly strong examples.

14. CARELESS DAUGHTERS

1. M. Mehta and Maitreyi Krishna Raj, "Survey of working women postgraduate science degree holders in Bombay"; and "Survey of non-working postgraduate science degree holders in Bombay," 1979–1981. Bombay: Shrimati Nathibai Damodar Thackersey University monograph, 1982.
2. *India Today*, September 30, 1987, 40.
3. Kalpana Bardhan, "Women's Work, Welfare, and Status," *Economic and Political Weekly* 20, no. 50 (December 14, 1985): 2211, 2214.
4. These were, as of 1988–1989, Sharad Joshi in Maharashtra and Swami Agnivesh.

15. A FOUR-THOUSAND-YEAR-OLD HISTORY

1. Kathryn Hansen, "The *Virangana* in North Indian History," *Economic and Political Weekly* 23, no. 18 (April 30, 1988).
2. See Erik Erikson, *Gandhi's Truth*, and Madhu Kishwar, "Gandhi on Women," *Economic and Political Weekly* 20, no. 40 (October 5, 12, 1985).
3. A *Directory of Women's Studies in India* was first published in 1986 by the Institute of Social Studies Trust, New Delhi.
4. André Béteille, "Elites, Status Groups, and Castes in Modern India," cited by Richard Lannoy, *The Speaking Tree*, 257.

CODA

1. Gita Sen, "Ethics in Third World Development, a Feminist Perspective" (The Rama Mehta Lecture, delivered at Radcliffe College, Cambridge, Mass., April 28, 1988). See also Gita Sen and Karen Crown, *Development, Crises, and Alternative Visions, Third World Women's Perspectives* (New York: Monthly Review Press, 1987) and Vandana Shiva, *Staying Alive: Women, Ecology and Survival in India* (London: Zed Press, 1988).

Bibliography

SECONDARY SOURCES

Ali Baigh, Tara. *India's Woman Power*. New Delhi: S. Chand, 1976.

Altekar, A. S. *The Position of Women in Hindu Civilisation*. New Delhi: Motilal Banarsidass, 1959.

Bardhan, Kalpana. "Women's Work, Welfare and Status, Forces of Tradition and Change in India." *Economic and Political Weekly*, 20, 50(1985): 2207–2220; 51–52: 2261–2268.

Basham, Arthur L. *The Wonder That Was India*. New York: Grove Press, 1959.

Béteille, André. *Caste, Class, and Power*. Berkeley: University of California Press, 1971.

Blaise, Clark, and Bharati Mukherjee. *Days and Nights in Calcutta*. New York: Doubleday, 1977.

Blumberg, Rhoda L., and Leela Dwaraki. *India's Educated Women*. New Delhi: Hindustan Publishing Corp., 1980.

Chanana, Karuna, ed. *Socialisation, Education and Women*. New Delhi: Orient Longman, 1988.

Chipp, Sylvia P., and Justin J. Green, eds. *Asian Women in Transition*. University Park: Pennsylvania State University Press, 1980.

Coomaraswamy, Ananda. *The Dance of Shiva*. New York: Farrar, Strauss, 1957.

Cormack, Margaret. *The Hindu Woman*. Bombay: Asia Publishing House, 1961.

———. *She Who Rides a Peacock*. Bombay: Asia Publishing House, 1961.

Das, Veena. "The Goddess and the Demon, an Analysis of the Devi Mahatmya." *Manushi* 30(1985): 28–32.

Desai, Anita. *Voices in the City*. New Delhi: Vision Books, 1965.

Desai, A. R. *Women's Liberation and Politics of Religious Personal Laws in India*. Bombay: Shah Memorial Trust, 1986.

Deshpande, Shashi. *That Long Silence*. London: Virago, 1988.

de Souza, Alfred, ed. *Women in Contemporary India*. New Delhi: Manohar, 1975.

Dimmitt, Cornelia, and J. A. B. van Buitenen, eds. and trans. *Classical Hindu Mythology*. Philadelphia: Temple University Press, 1978.

Dumont, Louis. *Homo Hierarchicus*. Chicago: University of Chicago Press, 1970.

Eck, Diana L. *Darśan, Seeing the Divine Image in India.* Chambersburg, Pa.: Anima Books, 1981.
Eliade, Mircea. *Le Sacré et le Profane.* Paris: Gallimard, 1965.
Erikson, Erik H. *Gandhi's Truth.* New York: Norton, 1969.
Everett, Jana M. *Women and Social Change in India.* New York: St. Martin's, 1979.
Gandhi, Mohandas K. *Autobiography.* New York: Dover, 1983.
Gulati, Leela. *Profiles in Female Poverty.* Oxford: Pergamon Press, 1982.
Hansen, Kathryn, "The *Virangana* in North Indian History." *Economic and Political Weekly* 23, no. 18(1988): WS25–33.
Hauswirth, Frieda (Das). *Purdah, the Status of Indian Women.* New York: Vanguard, 1932.
Isaacs, Harold R. *India's Ex-Untouchables.* New York: Harper & Row, 1974.
Jacobson, Doranne, and Susan S. Wadley. *Women in India.* New Delhi: Manohar, 1977.
Jain, Devaki. *Women's Quest for Power.* New Delhi: Vikas, 1980.
Jain, Devaki, and Nirmala Banerjee, eds. *Tyranny of the Household.* New Delhi: Vikas, 1985.
Kakar, Sudhir. *The Inner World.* Oxford: Oxford University Press, 1982.
———. *Shamans, Mystics and Doctors.* New York: Knopf, 1982.
Kakar, Sudhir, and Kamla Chowdhry. *Conflict and Choice, Indian Youth in a Changing Society.* Bombay: Somaiya, 1970.
Kali for Women, eds. *Truth Tales.* London: The Women's Press, 1986.
Kapur, Promilla. *Love, Marriage, Sex and the Indian Woman.* New Delhi: Vision Books, 1976.
———. *Conflict Between Adolescent Girls and Parents in India.* New Delhi: Vision Books, 1982.
Khanna, Girija, and Mariamma A. Verghese. *Indian Women Today.* New Delhi: Vikas, 1978.
Kinsley, David. *Hindu Goddesses.* Berkeley: University of California Press, 1988.
———. *The Sword and the Flute.* Berkeley: University of California Press, 1975.
Kishwar, Madhu. "Gandhi on Women." *Economic and Political Weekly* 20, no. 40 (1985): 1691–1702; 20, no. 41 (1985): 1753–1758.
Kishwar, Madhu, and Ruth Vanita. *In Search of Answers.* London: Zed Books, 1984.
Krishna Raj, Maitreyi. "Approaches to Self-Reliance for Women: Some Urban Models." Bombay: SNDT University Monograph, 1980.
Kynch, Jocelyn, and Amartya Sen. "Indian Women: Well-being and Survival." *Cambridge Journal of Economics* 7 (1983): 363–380.
Lannoy, Richard. *The Speaking Tree.* London: Oxford University Press, 1974.
Lebra, Joyce, J. Paulson, and Jana M. Everett, eds. *Women and Work in India.* New Delhi: Promilla & Co., 1984.
Liddle, Joanna, and Rama Joshi. *Daughters of Independence.* London: Zed Books, 1986.

Mayur, Rashmi, and P. R. Vohra, eds. *Bombay by 2000 A.D.* Bombay: Vohras Enterprises, 1986.

Mehta, M., and Maitreyi Krishna Raj. "Survey of Working Women Postgraduate Science Degree Holders in Bombay," and "Survey of Non-working Postgraduate Science Degree Holders in Bombay, 1979–1981." Bombay: Research Unit on Women's Studies Monograph, SNDT University, 1982.

Mehta, Rama. *The Western-Educated Indian Woman*. Bombay: Asia Publishing House, 1970.

———. *The Divorced Hindu Woman*. New Delhi: Vikas, 1975.

Mies, Maria. *Indian Women and Patriarchy*. New Delhi: Concept Publishing Co., 1980.

Mukherjee, Prabhati. *Hindu Women, Normative Models*. New Delhi: Orient Longman, 1978.

O'Flaherty, Wendy Doniger, trans. *Hindu Myths*. New York: Viking Penguin, 1975.

Olsen, Tillie. *Silences*. New York: Dell, 1978.

Omvedt, Gail. *We Will Smash This Prison!* London: Zed Books, 1980.

Patel, Vibhuti. *Reaching for Half the Sky*. Baroda: Antar Rashtriya Prakashan, 1985.

Ratté, Lou. "Goddesses, Mothers, and Heroines: Hindu Women and the Feminine in the Early Nationalist Movement." In *Women, Religion, and Social Change*, ed. Yvonne Y. Haddad and Ellison B. Findly. Albany: State University of New York Press, 1985.

Robinson, Sandra P. "Hindu Paradigms of Women: Images and Values." In *Women, Religion, and Social Change*, ed. Yvonne Y. Haddad and Ellison B. Findly. Albany: State University of New York Press, 1985.

Ross, Aileen. *The Hindu Family in its Urban Setting*. Toronto: University of Toronto Press, 1962.

Roy, Monisha. *Bengali Women*. Chicago: University of Chicago Press, 1972.

Shakti Editorial Collective. *In Search of Our Bodies*. Bombay: Shakti Trust, 1987.

Somjee, Geeta. *Narrowing the Gender Gap*. London: Macmillan, 1989.

Srinivas, M. N. *Social Change in Modern India*. New Delhi: Orient Longman, 1972.

Thapar, Romila. *A History of India (Vol. 1)*. Baltimore: Penguin, 1966.

Tindall, Gillian. *City of Gold*. Hounslow, Middlesex: Temple Smith, 1982.

Vitsaxis, Vassilis G. *Hindu Epics, Myths and Legends in Popular Illustration*. New Delhi: Oxford University Press, 1977.

Wadley, Susan S., ed. *The Powers of Tamil Women*. Syracuse: Syracuse University Press, 1980.

Zaehner, R. C. *Hinduism*. London: Oxford University Press, 1962.

———, ed. and trans. *Hindu Scriptures*. London: Dent [Everyman's Library], 1984.

Zimmer, Heinrich. *The Art of Indian Asia*. New York: Pantheon, 1948.

———. *Myths and Symbols in Indian Art and Civilization*. New York: Pantheon, 1946.

CLASSICAL SOURCES

Mahabharata. Translated by P. C. Roy. Calcutta: Oriental Publishing Co., 1919–1935.
———. Translated by P. P. S. Sastri. Madras: V. Ramaswamy Sastrulu, 1931.
———. Translated by J. A. B. van Buitenen. Vols. 1–3. Chicago: University of Chicago Press, 1971–1978.
———. Translated, selected, and condensed by R. K. Narayan. New Delhi: Hind Pocket Books, 1978.
The Laws of Manu. Translated by G. Buhler. In *Sacred Books of the East*, ed. F. Max Muller. 25. Oxford: Oxford University Press, 1879–1900.
The Lay of the Anklet (Silappadigaram). Translated by V. R. R. Dikshitar. Oxford, 1939.
Ramayana. Translated by H. P. Shastri. London: Shantisadan, 1962.
———. Translated, selected, and condensed by C. Rajagopalachari. Bombay: Bharatiya Vidya Bhavan, 1980.

OTHER SOURCES CONSULTED

Economic and Political Weekly (1980–1990)
India Today (1985–1990)
Manushi, a Journal about Women and Society (1979– 1990)

Newspapers

The Hindu
Hindustan Times
Indian Express
The Statesman
The Times of India

Index